NO SOLDIER LEFT BEHIND

THE LIFE AND TIMES OF BRIGADIER GENERAL
JOHN G. KULHAVI, USAF, RET.

THE LEGACY BOOK SERIES

DON STEELE, PH.D

To those warriors who bravely fought in the military; to those who want to create a better world for others through an entrepreneurial spirit; to those who are willing to forsake the "me-first" attitude in the name of love; and to present and future generations of John Kulhavi's family.

INTRODUCTION

In interviews with people who fought with John in Vietnam, he is most remembered for his commitment to "No soldier left behind." In his over-three-hundred combat missions, many involved transporting wounded or dying soldiers from battle fields.

The adage "No soldier left behind," spawned several centuries ago, exemplifies what the American people and the military feel is due to those who have made the ultimate sacrifice. This ethos is even embedded in the Airman's Creed ("I will never leave an Airman behind.") and the Soldier's Creed ("I will never leave a fallen comrade.").

"No soldier left behind" can also be seen

as an extension of "Do to others what you would have them do to you." I wouldn't want to be left behind enemy lines, abandoned, alone, wounded, or dead. I would want to return home to family, friends, loved ones, or people that care that I ever existed.

John Kulhavi abides by this expressed commitment to leaving no soldier behind. He stays true to the military values of personal responsibility, duty, honor, and faith. He created a personal vow–a mental picture fueled by passion:

My word is my life, and my life is my word.

AUTHOR'S NOTES

When an old man dies, a library burns to the ground. The world is denied his learning.
    African Proverb

When the light shines the brightest and the pressure is the highest, only the strongest will survive and thrive. John Kulhavi does not look like a military hero, a very successful entrepreneur, or a venture capitalist and philanthropist. He appears to be everyman. Yet, as they say, "looks can be deceiving." Retired Brigadier General John G. Kulhavi is all of the above. He has what many would call "the *it* factor."

In this book, John reveals much of his

public and private life, sharing essential wisdom and knowledge through a series of intimate conversations with me. In addition, I conducted many interviews with others who have been a significant part of John's life.

John Kulhavi and I were roommates at Central Michigan University (CMU). I earned my bachelor of science and master of arts degrees from CMU and my PhD from The Ohio State University. John earned two bachelor's degrees, a teaching certificate, and a Reserve Officers' Training Corps (ROTC) commission as second lieutenant. We were also Phi Sigma Epsilon fraternity brothers.

John and I embarked on very divergent career paths after completing our undergraduate degrees at CMU. He entered the military after he earned his second lieutenant bars through the CMU Reserve Officer Training Program (ROTC). While serving as a helicopter pilot in Vietnam, he flew over three hundred combat missions. Throughout his military career, he earned two Distinguished Flying Cross awards, a Purple Heart, a Legion of Merit award, twenty-two Air Medals, a Bronze Star, and sixteen other awards. The capstone of his military career was earning the rank of brigadier general.

After John retired from the US Army, he served in the Army Reserve and became a financial advisor for Merrill Lynch. While at Merrill Lynch, he created the first financial advisory team in the brokerage industry. How this happened is very interesting.

When John suggested to his Detroit bosses that he create a team rather than continuing as a lone broker, he was met with "That's not the way we do things around here" by his boss. Because of his deep commitment to teamwork that he found necessary as a helicopter team captain, he refused to accept that response. Instead, he traveled on his own dime to Washington D.C. to meet with the chairman of the board of Merrill Lynch, Donald Regan (the same Donald Regan who later served as secretary of the treasury and chief of staff under President Ronald Reagan). Regan had served in the United States Marine Corps, so John was quite confident that Regan felt as strongly as he did about the value of teamwork.

Regan listened to John's request and quickly said, "Do it! I will inform your Detroit office that I support your request." Upon returning to Detroit, John started forming his team. His team soon led Merrill Lynch in the midwest region of the United States in sales and profitability for many years. His team also scored extremely high in the national rankings. Within Merrill Lynch, teams are now the common modus operandi.

John earned several individual honors while at Merrill Lynch. He was honored many times in *Barron's* special report of their Top 100 Financial Advisors and Top 100 US Stockbrokers.

After retiring from Merrill Lynch, John became a successful entrepreneur, an investor, and a philanthropist. He has donated millions of dollars to the Central Michigan University's neuroscience program, ROTC programs, and the athletic department. Two buildings now carry his name at his alma mater. Several different venues are also named after John Kulhavi: the basketball court in the events center, a residence hall, a room in Park Library, a room in the College of Business Administration, a laboratory in the Beaver Island Biological Station, a room in the Education Building, and a room in the Health Professions Building.

John and I lost track of each other for many years. We re-connected when I served as the keynote motivational speaker at a Merrill Lynch management event. John was in the audience. We chatted after my speech. That brief chat became a new chapter in both of our lives. Among other things, we reunited as members of Phi Sigma Epsilon.

It's an honor to capture the life and times of a man who overcomes every obstacle that gets in his way. This military warrior used his fearless approach to battle in all aspects of his life.

PART I:
THE INDUSTRIOUS NATURE OF JOHN KULHAVI

Rex Gibson, a lifelong friend of John's, stated, "John and I were always buddies. One thing I really remember about John was that he was industrious. He would buy something and find a way to make cash out of it. He has always been diligent and hardworking so I can see why he has had success throughout his life."

CHAPTER 1
IN THE BEGINNING

John Kulhavi was born on October 22, 1942. His grandparents on his father's side immigrated from Yugoslavia. His mother was Polish. John was their firstborn, followed in order by the birth of his brother, Larry; sister, Sharon; and brother, Don. Later, his mom gave birth to his half-sister, Kathy.

John's early childhood was spent in the mostly-Polish-Catholic community of Hamtramck, Michigan. Hamtramck featured forty-three private bars and clubs, five or six movie theaters, and great stores all within the two-and-a-half-mile strip along the main street in town. John says, "When I got old enough, I would take my three-dollar allowance and go shop at the stores on Campau Street. At that time, three dollars would go a long way."

A week before his thirteenth birthday, John's family moved to Skidway Lake, a small community in northern Michigan. Skidway Lake (hereafter referred to as Skidway) had a population of three hundred local residents in the winter months and ballooned up to over ten thousand tourists in the summer (in on Memorial Day; out on Labor Day). During the off-season, hunters, fishermen, and snowmobile enthusiasts visited the Skidway area.

The transition from Hamtramck to Skidway was a major change in John's life. Hamtramck was a busy, bustling town, while Skidway consisted of one stoplight and a few mom-and-pop businesses. John said a tourist once told him, "I plugged in my electric razor and the street lights dimmed." John adds, "I am absolutely certain that the toothbrush was invented at Skidway Lake; if it were invented anywhere else, it would have been called 'the teethbrush.'"

The choice to move the family to Skidway was decided when John's father visited the area and fell in love with northern Michigan. John's mother opened a small grocery store, while John's father got a job in a small tool-and-die company three to four miles out of town. John loved the passion his mom had for her store and he worked at the store from the day it opened all the way through his college years.

"Mom's store was never profitable," John remembers. "My mom was the most kind-hearted and generous person. Most customers would come and give her a sob story and she would allow them to buy their groceries on credit. She gave way too much away. And, unfortunately, most of the people that bought on credit never paid their bills. In spite of this, they never hesitated to come back and buy more items on credit. To this day I still have a book in my house of all the names of people who owed her money for groceries."

There is no doubt in my mind that John's heartfelt giving comes from his mothers's modeling of such behavior. When his wife Carole offers that John is sometimes too trusting in business ventures, it is a manifestation of the credulous influence his mother had on his life.

John says, "Our store ownership only lasted for a few years before Mom had to sell it. She didn't make enough money from the sale to pay back the debt she owed. A nice couple, the Coopers, ended up buying the store, but they knew nothing about business, so I came with the store. They paid me fifty cents an hour to work there.

"Shortly after the store was sold, Dad packed up and left Mom. We didn't have a nickel to our name. There were a total of five of us living in a one-bedroom cabin. Being the eldest, I tried to help Mom make ends meet. On top of working at the store, I would often find odd jobs that allowed me to bring home some money so we could afford bread and eggs. I would recruit my brother to clean up the beer and pop cans left behind by the flatlanders [a term 'Up-North' residents used to label the summer tourists in northern Michigan]. I also remember shooting deer or picking up roadkill to butcher and sell for thirty dollars. That was a lot of money in 1957." John's later military commitment, "Leave no soldier behind," can be attributed to the fact that his father had left him behind, causing John and the whole family a great deal of pain.

John related that the most memorable job he ever had occurred when he was sixteen:

> I remember the whole thing like it was yesterday. I saw an ad in the *Ogemaw County Herald* saying they were hiring a driver that could drive five individuals from West Branch to Traverse City for twenty dollars. The ad said all that was needed was a car and a valid driver's license. Gas back then was thirty-three cents a gallon. I did the math and figured out I would make a fourteen-dollar profit. I told Mom we could buy milk and eggs for three weeks with that much money.
>
> I got permission to borrow the car and drove into West Branch to find out that there was some information missing from the ad: My job was to transport five cognitively and/or

emotionally impaired individuals. Had I known this, I would have bypassed this opportunity. But all in all, it was a job and I went with it.

About halfway there, one of them said, "I have to pee—now!" I hurried to pull over and went into a store to explain the situation to the clerk. Thankfully, she let him use the bathroom and I waited for him to be done. We walked back out to the car and the other four passengers were GONE!

I hit panic mode, realizing I had just lost my four passengers on the streets in Kalkaska. Why they ever allowed a sixteen-year-old to do this job I have no idea, because it would never fly today.

I took the one guy I still had with me by the hand and started to search up and down the aisle of every store on the main street. Once we found one [missing person], we would grab a hold of his hand, forming a train that ultimately included all five people. Finally, two-and-a-half hours later, we were ready to get back in the car.

One of the people I was transporting had pockets full of suckers. On his unsupervised portion of the trip, he had stolen a whole bunch of suckers from one of the stores. I swear, this guy had to have eaten fifty suckers, one right after another, from Kalkaska to Traverse City.

I dropped my passengers off in Traverse City, drove back to West Branch, got my money, and told them not to count on me to come back for this job ever again.

CHAPTER 2
STRIVING TO FIT IN AT WHITTEMORE-PRESCOTT HIGH SCHOOL

Living in Skidway was a lot different than living in his birth town of Hamtramck, Michigan. It was a small town and John quickly found out that everyone knew everyone, including everyone's business.

It didn't take very long before John figured out that if he wanted to be a part of the "in-group" of teens at Whittemore-Prescott High School, then he had to play sports. Even though he weighed a mere 120 pounds, he tried out for the football, baseball, basketball, and track teams. John was an average athlete and he successfully made the roster of all four teams, although, as John points out, "anybody who went out for those teams made it because the school needed players. None of the coaches ever made cuts." It was like John to invest time and energy in learning about teamwork and engaging fully, whether his talent seemed to measure up or not. In every sense, he was a true grinder, willing to work harder than others to better himself and help the teams he became a part of. The following song by John Fogerty is entitled "Centerfield." The line, "put me in coach," appears to apply in John's case.

"Centerfield" by John Fogerty

> *Well, I beat the drum and hold the phone*
> *The sun came out today*
> *We're born again, there's new grass on the field*
> *A-roundin' third, I'm headed for home*
> *It's a brown-eyed handsome man*
> *Anyone can understand the way I feel*

*Oh, put me in coach, I'm ready to
    play today
Put me in coach, I'm ready to play
    today
Look at me, I can be centerfield*

*Well, I spent some time in the
    Mudville Nine
Watching it from the bench
You know I took some lumps
When the Mighty Casey
    struck out
So say, "Hey Willie, tell Ty Cobb
    and Joe DiMaggio"
Don't say it ain't so you know the
    time is now*

*So put me in coach, I'm ready to
    play today
Put me in coach, I'm ready to play
    today
Look at me, I can be centerfield*

*You got a beat-up glove, a home-
    made bat
And a brand new pair of shoes
You know I think it's time to give*

this game a ride
Just to hit the ball an' touch 'em
all, a moment in the sun
It's-a gone and you can tell that
one goodbye

Oh, put me in coach, I'm ready to
play today
Put me in coach, I'm ready to play
today
Look at me, I can be centerfield

Oh, put me in coach, I'm ready to
play today
Put me in coach, I'm ready to play
today
Look at me, gotta be centerfield
Yeah

John remembers playing junior varsity basketball: "I was only allowed in the game if the team was up by twenty points and there was a minute left. I played three-and-a-half minutes the entire season. I knew basketball was not my sport, but I showed my teammates I was 'all in.'

"When I went out for baseball, our

coach figured out a motto: 'When Kulhavi pitches, everybody hits.'" John played second base and was occasionally called in to pitch.

Football was John's second-favorite sport. "I was a starter in football. That didn't require a lot. On offense I played half-back and on defense I played safety. I also played the clarinet in high school. We had four clarinet players in the band; I was the fourth chair. But the good part was that no one ever challenged me for my chair. At halftime, I would go to the locker room, take off my football uniform, put on my marching band uniform, and go out and perform. Then I would switch again, and go out and play the last half of the game."

John performed well on the track team for Whittemore-Prescott:

> Track was my favorite sport. I was the shortest guy on the track team. My coach, in his infinite wisdom, decided to make me a hurdler. My initial thought was that he might as well teach me pole-vaulting, because that

was the only way I was going to get over those hurdles.

I really took track seriously. I usually would eat dry toast and hot tea the day before and the day of the meet. However, our last meet of my senior year was a different story. This was our biggest meet of the season. The seniors were going to graduate in a couple days so we just wanted to get the meet over with. We had a party the night before. I'm not much of a beer drinker, but I drank a bottle or two. We stayed up until about 3:30 in the morning and slept maybe two or three hours.

Once we got on the school bus, some players smoked cigars and cigarettes on the way to the meet. There was about an hour and a half before the first heat of hurdles, so three other guys and myself walked a mile to a restaurant. We had cheeseburgers, chili, and milkshakes.

I got back just in time for the first heat and I ended up winning it. Not only did this surprise me, but my coach and the entire team were surprised. Then, about thirty minutes later, I ran in the semi-finals and won that heat. At that point, no one could figure out what was happening. I was running better than I ever had the entire season. Then came the finals, and I didn't win it; I ended up placing second. This tied the high school record for the 180-yard low hurdles that had been held for thirteen years. Perhaps the cheeseburgers and milkshake before the race helped me run better than the dry toast I had eaten every race prior.

John's first girlfriend in high school was Nancy, but there were challenges. It was no secret to the community that John's mother was struggling to make ends meet and John was the child of divorced parents. As John tells it, "Back then there was a stigma around divorced parents and their kids. Unfortunately, children of divorce were looked down upon. I never quite understood that because I had nothing to do with my parents' divorce—I was fifteen years old."

One night, Nancy broke off her relationship with John, breaking his heart. John said, "Everyone around me could tell I was devastated. One night, my mom decided enough was enough. She sat me down at the kitchen counter and said, 'John, I don't generally give you advice, but tonight I will. I know how you feel about Nancy. The advice I am going to give you is that the best way to forget about a girlfriend is to find a new girlfriend.' I said, 'What do you mean?' She said, 'You need to start dating.' She was absolutely right and her advice worked."

Years later, John found out the real reason Nancy broke up with him. According to his friend Keith Charters, Nancy had told him she had broken up with John because her father made her do it. He said, "You can't date John anymore; he's never going to amount to anything!"

Would John prove Nancy's father wrong?

CHAPTER 3
DADDY DEPARTS

It was during John's sophomore year of high school when his father left the family for another woman. After he departed, John says he and his father had very little contact. "I loved my dad. He taught me how to hunt and fish, but when he left my mom, he lost status in my life. He had left her with four kids and a one-bedroom cabin, nothing else." Like the phrase from the song, "Papa Was a Rollin' Stone," when he left, all he left them was alone.

"Papa was a Rollin' Stone" by The Temptations

It was the third of September
That day I'll always remember,
    yes I will
'Cause that was the day that my
    daddy died
I never got a chance to see him
Never heard nothin' but bad
    things about him
Momma I'm depending on you to
    tell me the truth
Momma just hung her head and
    said, son

Papa was a rolling stone
Wherever he laid his hat was
    his home
And when he died, all he left us
    was alone
Papa was a rolling stone (my son,
    yeah)
Wherever he laid his hat was
    his home
And when he died, all he left us
    was alone

Hey Momma!
Is it true what they say that Papa

never worked a day in his life
And Momma, some bad talk goin'
round town sayin' that
Papa had three outside children
And another wife, and that ain't
right
Heard some talk Papa doing some
storefront preachin'
Talking about saving souls and all
the time leechin'
Dealing in dirt, and stealing in
the name of the Lord
Momma just hung her head
and said

Papa was a rolling stone (my son)
Wherever he laid his hat was
his home
And when he died, all he left us
was alone
Hey Papa was a rolling stone (dad
gumma it)
Wherever he laid his hat was
his home
And when he died, all he left us
was alone

Hey Momma
I heard Papa called himself a jack-of-all-trades
Tell me is that what sent Papa to an early grave
Folks say Papa would beg, borrow, steal
To pay his bills
Hey Momma
Folks say Papa never was much on thinking
Spent most of his time chasing women and drinking
Momma I'm depending on you to tell me the truth
Momma looked up with a tear in her eye and said, son

Papa was a rolling stone (well, well, well, well)
Wherever he laid his hat was his home
And when he died, all he left us was alone (lone, lone, lone, alone)
Papa was a rolling stone

Wherever he laid his hat was
his home
And when he died, all he left us
was alone
Wherever he laid his hat was
his home
And when he died, all he left us
was alone
My daddy was
Papa was a rolling stone (yes he
was, yeah)
Wherever he laid his hat was
his home

"I remember my dad earned three strikes in my life that damaged our relationship. Leaving my mother was the first strike. The second strike came shortly after I turned sixteen." The third strike will be discussed later. "At this point, I had little contact with my father and his new girlfriend, Grace. However, I did go down and see him once in a while."

John says, "Grace had a '57 Chevy two-door hardtop and I *loved* that car. Grace and my dad had a cabin in Skidway and they would come up every so often. When they drove the car up north, I would wash and wax the car and shampoo the carpet. In return for cleaning and polishing, I was allowed to use the car if I had a date, or plans with my friends."

John's dad had promised him that if they ever got a new car, John would get the '57 Chevy since he loved it so much. One day, Grace and his dad drove up in a new car. Of course, John was expecting to get the Chevy. However, to his dismay they had traded it in. To this day, he hasn't forgotten that feeling of extreme disappointment.

"I made a life-changing commitment that day. I promised myself to never make a commitment that I could not live up to. My belief is, 'If your word is no good, you're no good.'"

As John's personal and professional friend, I have witnessed him keeping his commitments on many occasions. With John, his word is truly his bond. He has paid a big price when people took advantage of him, but he still remains devoted to keeping his commitments.

For example, one time a fraternity brother from back in his college days borrowed over $40,000 from John. While lying on his deathbed, he looked at John and asked, "Will you forgive that debt?" He died the next day, and John delivered his eulogy. John discovered later that his friend's wife had a $500,000 insurance policy and attained close to half-a-million more when she sold the house. John never received any of his money back, and never pursued the issue further. Sometimes there is a downside to keeping promises when the beneficiary doesn't share those same values.

During John's senior year of high school, his mother decided to move back to Hamtramck to work at City National Bank. John was not about to change schools right before starting his senior year, so he decided to move in with his Uncle Joe and his wife. A year later, Uncle Joe moved (after his wife passed away), and John had only a few months left before heading to college.

John says, "During this time, I would live out of my car. Every once in a while, I would sleep in the cabin. Thankfully, after a little while, the Coopers, who had bought the store from my mom, offered me a bedroom in the back of the store for free."

He worked many jobs to provide for himself and to make as much money as he could to get ready for college. He was working at the grocery store, selling real estate, and working for a construction company building cabins.

John recalls, "I was the littlest guy of the group and the youngest. There was this big dumb bully that worked in our group. He was always jabbing at me and making fun of me. Although I was this little guy, my job was to carry eighty-pound bundles of shingles up the ladder and onto the roof. And one day, I'm up on the roof. I had just carried up a bundle of shingles when he picked up a big two-by-four, hit me in the rear end, and tried to knock me off the roof. I could have fallen and broken my back and neck, but he didn't care. He was laughing as he climbed back down off the roof. I yelled, 'You dumb son-of-a-bitch.' That really pissed him off and he said, 'Okay little guy, we're going to see how you fly.' He started up the ladder. I only had access to one way down, and that happened to be the same way he was coming up.

"I knew he was mean enough that, if he

had gotten up there, he would have thrown me off the roof. I grabbed a claw hammer and I moved close to the top of the ladder, looking down as he was climbing up. As soon as his hand reached the roof, I hammered his hand as hard as I could. His eyes got really big and I said, 'Come on asshole, the next one's going to get you right in the head.' He went back down the ladder and someone took him to the West Branch Hospital. I had broken his hand and three or four fingers. Somebody once told me, 'If you're dealing with somebody crazy, the only way that they will leave you alone is to do something that convinces them that you're crazier than they are.' I believe there's some truth to that. After breaking his hand, he never messed with me again. In fact, he treated me very well from that time forward. I might add, everybody did. They all thought I was crazy as a loon."

The song, "Crazy as a Loon" by John Prine, exemplifies this story quite well.

"Crazy as a Loon" by John Prine

Back before I was a movie star
Straight off of the farm
I had a picture of another
   man's wife
Tattooed on my arm

With a pack of Camel cigarettes
In the sleeve of my T-shirt
I'm headin' out to Hollywood
Just to have my feelings hurt

That town will make you crazy
Just give it a little time
You'll be walking 'round in circles
Down at Hollywood and Vine

You'll be waitin' on a phone call
At the wrong end of a broom
Yes, that town'll make you crazy
Crazy as a loon

So, I headed down to Nashville
To become a country star
Every night you'd find me
   hangin'
At every honky-tonkin' bar

Pretty soon I met a woman
Pretty soon she done me wrong
Pretty soon my life got sadder
Than any country song

That town will make you crazy
Just give it a little time
You'll be walking 'round in circles
Lookin' for that country rhyme

You'll be waitin' on a phone call
At the wrong end of a broom
Yeah, that town'll make you crazy
Crazy as a loon

So, I gathered up my savvy
Bought myself a business suit
I headed up to New York City
Where a man can make some loot

I got hired Monday morning
Downsized that afternoon
Overcome with grief that evening
Now I'm crazy as a loon

So I'm up here in the North
    Woods

Just staring at a lake
Wondering just exactly how much
They think a man can take

I eat fish to pass the time away
'Neath this blue Canadian moon
This old world has made me crazy
Crazy as a loon

Lord, this world will make you
    crazy
Crazy as a loon

As the summer came to an end, John packed up his car to start a new chapter of his life. He would be beginning his freshman year at Central Michigan University.

CHAPTER 4
JOHN'S COLLEGE YEARS

"Central Michigan University [CMU], was the option I chose for college," John recalls. "It wasn't a huge decision regarding where I wanted to go to college. I already knew it was going to be CMU for three reasons: one, my best friend, Keith Charters, who was one year ahead of me, was there; two, they accepted me; and three, it was a university I felt I could afford to attend.

"Picking my major was fairly easy...or so I thought. In high school, I maintained a B-average and my mom was certain I should be a doctor. To make her proud, I started in pre-med. I quickly felt that perhaps I didn't have the intellect; I didn't like dissecting cats or any of my chemistry or biology classes; and I certainly didn't have the money. I ended my pre-med journey and I decided my junior year to switch to psychology."

When starting college, John's relationship with his father was rocky but there was the faintest glimmer of a relationship and respect shared between them. Probably out of guilt, John's dad decided to foot the bill for John to go to college. This offer did not work out as planned.

John says, "After my first semester at CMU, my dad got 'strike three' in our fading relationship, and from that day forward, I tolerated him and tried to treat him how any son should treat their father. However, the little respect I had left for him as a man soon ended. This happened when I left school to go see him one weekend and we ended up in an argument. I still remember his words to me: 'You'll never make it through college without me.' I looked him square in the eyes and said, 'Don't bet on it,' and I got up and walked straight out of his house."

The lesson here is that sometimes the people who are never supposed to disappoint you do just that. The relationship becomes toxic. When this happens, the following advice comes to mind: "When you're riding a dead horse—get off."

This was the third strike in John's relationship with his father and the second time John had been challenged with the possibility that he wouldn't be successful (Nancy's father was the first). Although he didn't know what Nancy's father had said at that moment in his life, John knew that everyone looked at him as if the odds were never going to be in his favor. This served as motivation for John.

Cognitive psychology tells us that *we move toward and become like that which we think about—whether it's good for us or not.* Due to those comments suggesting he'd never make it, John was bound and determined to prove both Nancy's father and his own father that they were dead wrong. Whether it was inspiration or desperation that drove John, even he doesn't know. What he did know was that he would prove them wrong.

John says, "Throughout my high school and college years, I never had any less than three jobs [at one time], and at one point I was working five to try and make ends meet for myself. I was not going to let myself fail. I couldn't afford living in the dorms at CMU, so I rented a bed on Mrs. Birdhill's back porch for five dollars a week. She rented to six of us guys: four were upstairs and two of us slept on the porch. The porch was not insulated and we slept on World War I bunks. This was an old house and it had one bathroom for the six of us—it worked for us most of the time. In times of urgency, we did what was necessary outside.

"My diet was both inexpensive and unhealthy. I religiously ate Kraft Mac and Cheese and hot dogs. Fortunately, we all liked this stuff. There was one exception when it came to meals: Every Monday, Keith Charters would make a big pot of spaghetti. That pot of spaghetti would sit on the stove from Monday through Friday afternoon. The guys would come in and heat it up. It was never placed in the refrigerator. Whatever was left on Friday, Keith would dump out, and the next Monday he would make another pot of spaghetti."

One of the stupidest things that John admits he ever did happened while living in that house:

I had a car, but it was in rough condition. It didn't have brakes, it didn't have turn signals; it had one headlight and a whole slew of other things wrong with it. However, I needed a car to go back to Skidway, because I still worked weekends at the store and my new girlfriend was a year behind me and still a senior in high school. I also really loved that car; it was one of my favorites. One day, Keith asked me to take him to the laundromat, and we were almost home when a police car began to follow me. I made it back to the old lady's house and I pulled into the driveway, hoping the policeman would drive by.

Unfortunately, the policeman pulled in right behind us. Keith got out with his laundry bag and walked in the house to leave me alone with the officer. I started to ask the officer what I did wrong when all three guys, from within the house, started yelling at the cop to check different things on my car. The officer did, and he found about forty reasons to write me a ticket. I lived off a few dollars a week—there wasn't any way I could afford to pay for that hefty ticket. I guess the officer decided to give me a break and he said, "I don't want to write you a ticket so I won't, but if I ever see this car on the road again without a bill for all of the repairs, I will write you for everything." He got in his car and drove away.

I was a young and naive freshman, so what did I do? I kept driving to work at the store and to see my girlfriend. But I wasn't dumb. I strategized that I could keep on driving the car as long as I would never go through town or drive on the highway. I stuck to the back and side roads.

One day, I was on my way back to the store and I saw the same police car. We passed each other and made eye contact, and I knew he recognized me immediately. That is when I did the stupidest thing ever. The policeman whips his car around and I put the pedal to the metal in my old rattletrap. I cut my car hard to the right and went straight through a cornfield. In my rearview mirror, I could see the officer standing outside his car with his hands on his hips, staring at me. I chuckled to myself, thinking I got away, only to be met at the edge of the field by a farmer and his 12-gauge shotgun. I started to explain everything that had happened and how I didn't have money to fix the car. The farmer asked, "How much money do you have on you?" I pulled out the last bit of money I had in my pocket and counted it. I said, "I have three dollars and twenty-seven cents." He looked at me, grabbed the money, and left me with not a penny to my name.

I got back to Skidway, parked the car, and never drove it again. I had no money for a new car, so I had to start hitchhiking every weekend back and forth between Mount Pleasant and Skidway. I had made a commitment to the store that I was not backing out of, and so I was stuck hitchhiking for the rest of my college experience.

John's dad did try to reconnect with him from time to time, but John looked at every conversation as nothing more than a lecture about how to live his life. "I was nineteen, and for four years he wasn't in my life and I was doing just fine on my own. I didn't need a lecture from him at that point. I will say that a little while after our fight, when I started paying for my own college costs, he started mailing me twenty bucks a week. I never took the money. I would readdress it and send the money back to his house. I was determined to make it on my own financially. I would struggle before taking handouts from a man who didn't respect me and was counting on my failure."

During another semester in college, John lived upstairs in a house that he and his friends called "Tombstone Territory," probably because tombstones were all over the yard. The owners of the house, an elderly couple, lived downstairs. John, two other guys, and I (Don Steele) shared the upstairs. A couple weekends a month, the owner of the house and his wife would pack up and go to visit one of their daughters. As soon as they would pull out of the driveway, I would run downstairs, pick the lock to their house, unplug their TV, carry it upstairs, and plug it in. We would therefore have the use of their TV for the entire weekend. On Sunday afternoon while the guys watched TV, John would have to watch the window. As soon as the owner pulled into the driveway on Sunday evening, John would run downstairs and engage him and his wife in a conversation to delay them from entering the house for a couple minutes. That way, I could get the TV back downstairs and plug it in.

"During my sophomore year," John remembers, "my friend Keith recruited me to join his fraternity, Phi Sigma Epsilon. I enjoyed the fraternity, and quickly became the president. I found I made friends pretty easily, and I really liked being in charge of the biggest fraternity on CMU's campus at the time.

"Later in life, when I saw the movie *Animal House*, I thought, 'Holy cow, they patterned this movie after our fraternity.' I ended up being the president of Phi Sigma Epsilon for five semesters, not because I was a great leader but because nobody else wanted the job. I had to appear in front of the dean of students on a regular basis and concoct some story to keep our fraternity from being kicked off campus for misconduct." John remembers many things that happened with the fraternity brothers that seemed to be funny at the time, but now looking back, perhaps they weren't.

Phi Sigma Epsilon was nearly kicked off campus in 1959. According to John's fraternity brother Bob Stuart, who pledged in the fall of 1959, the following story evolved. Bob was asked to serve as social chairman for the fraternity. When he asked an older frat brother, Jim Barry, what the social chairman does, his answer was, "Rent a hall, get a keg of beer, and buy some potato chips and pretzels." Bob asked Barry, "And that's it?"

Barry said, "Yup, that's it!" Bob asked, "How do I advertise this?" and Barry responded, "Just tell one brother!" According to Bob, "The party was a great success—enjoyed by all."

After the party, it was realized that the state police had taken the license numbers of all the people at the party. Bob Stuart and Dick Dexter, who was the fraternity president at the time, were summoned to meet with Dean Sorrell in his office. As a result of that meeting, the Phi Sigma Epsilon fraternity was banned from having any off-campus social events for the rest of the year. Such events included, but were not limited to, the annual tug-of-war contest and the canoe race. In addition, a letter was sent to all parents of the frat members informing them of the event and subsequent sanctions that were rendered by the dean's office.

In spite of the sanctions, the Phi Sigma Epsilon brothers continued to push the envelope of acceptable fraternity behavior. Some of this was due to the fact that several military veterans were members and they did not pay much attention to the rules and regulations.

In another example, John states, "A story that comes to mind is what I remember as 'The Bus Story.' Back then, it was mandatory to do two years of ROTC for all male students in any state-supported college. There were fourteen state-supported colleges in Michigan. Central Michigan University was one of them. They gave you an army uniform and a badge that said 'ROTC' (Reserve Officer Training Corps). I learned early that wearing the ROTC uniform was beneficial. For example, when I hitchhiked, I always got picked up sooner than if I wasn't wearing the uniform. People respected service guys.

"On one occasion, three [fraternity] brothers wanted to buy beer, but they didn't have any money. With their ROTC uniforms on, they went to the Mount Pleasant public school bus yard. They hot-wired a small school bus and drove it to Lansing, which is about sixty-five miles away. Then they pulled up to the Greyhound station, sat behind the wheel, and said, 'Bus to Mount Pleasant leaves in ten minutes.' About six people boarded the bus and they charged them two dollars each. They drove them to the Greyhound station in Mount Pleasant. They disembarked the passengers, and then parked the bus back where they had found it. The fares they collected gave them enough money to buy two cases of Carling Black Label beer, which was the cheapest beer they could buy. They didn't care; they just wanted beer."

In addition to the stories that John just shared, I have a personal one to include. I fondly remember one incident that involved frat brothers Dick Luther and Bob Peters. One day, Dick was trying to find Bob. Someone told him that Bob had said he was going to get a haircut. So Dick walked to the barber shop, stuck his head in the door, and yelled, "Bob Peters here?" The barber looked at Dick and said, "No. We just cut hair!"

The shenanigans continued at CMU and on other campuses. Eventually the Phi Sigma Epsilon charter was pulled at the national level. It somewhat resurrected itself but not at CMU under the name Phi Sigma Kappa.

John says, "While living in the fraternity house, I still worked three to five jobs but I was becoming more creative in my efforts to generate sources of revenue. My entrepreneurial spirit began to kick in.

"One day I thought, 'I'm living in a fraternity house with twenty-eight guys.' Do you know how many condoms twenty-eight guys use? Back in the day, if you wanted a condom, you had to go to the drug store and ask for one because they were under the counter. Usually there was a woman behind the counter and many of us were too embarrassed to buy one."

In the entrepreneurial world, the common mantra for success is "Find a need and fill it!" John saw there was a need and he set out to fill that need.

John's condom story reminds me of my trips from Saginaw to Mount Pleasant. My uncle, Jack Allison, owned a bar near Hemlock. I would stop in there on my way to and from campus. One day, Uncle Jack was tending bar, and a man walked out of the bathroom and whispered to Uncle Jack, "I put a dollar in the condom machine and nothing came out." Uncle Jack said, "I'll have to call the vendor and get that fixed." After the guy had left, we both laughed as Uncle Jack told me, "I have never put a condom in that machine. Almost anybody who tries to buy one is too embarrassed to tell me what happened. I make about $100 a month on that machine."

John says, "When I realized how much money I could make off these fraternity guys, I used what little money I had and bought a cigar box full of condoms."

One night when John and his frat brothers got together for dinner, John said, "Listen, there is a cigar box full of rubbers in my room. If you guys want one, you put a quarter in and take a rubber out. I do inventory every night and if I'm missing one quarter, you are going back to the drug store and buying them yourself from now on." From that day on, all the guys in the house bought condoms from him and he never missed a quarter. John didn't need them for himself, he just needed the money they brought in.

"About a week into my lucrative condom business, one of the fraternity brothers yelled to me and said, 'Hey, the rubbers you're selling us, are they guaranteed?' I stood up and said, 'They most certainly are. If one breaks and your girlfriend gets pregnant, you can bring it back to me and I'll give you a brand new one for free.' Everyone started laughing and I looked at the brother and said, 'You dumb shit. How can I guarantee the rubbers?'"

After John started having financial success from his condom sales, he decided to branch out a bit and bought a couple of inexpensive watches to sell them at a profit. He had discovered that many of his frat brothers liked to buy gifts for their girlfriends and John could make it easy for them to get these watches without having to go shopping, which most of the guys hated to do.

"Before long, I was making $100 a month from condom and watch sales. I did so well that I managed to pay for a whole semester of college off of that. As a side note, one night we had a frat party that included our girlfriends. It was amazing to see so many young ladies wearing the same watch."

Even though John was able to pay for a whole semester's-worth of school expenses with his condom and watch sales, he didn't make enough to buy a car. "I was still hitchhiking back and forth between Mount

Pleasant and Skidway to work at the store. A lot of the time I would be picked up by semi-truck drivers. One experience still sticks out to me in particular: This driver had picked me up. He drove in silence for a while until he asked if I was hungry. I was, but he was already giving me a ride and I didn't have the money for a meal, so I told him I would be okay until I got to where I was going. Luckily, the new owners of the store would allow me to eat from the store for free and still sleep in the room in the back of the store."

The truck driver looked at John and said, "I know you're hungry." After a brief argument put up on John's part, he pulled off and stopped at the Pinconning Cheese Shop and went inside. He left the truck running, so John just stayed inside where it was warm until he got back. He hopped back in the truck, holding a paper bag that contained a ring of pickled bologna, cheese, saltine crackers, potato chips, and a six-pack of Pepsi. He said "Eat!" and John did.

"I cannot explain how good that food tasted," John remembers. "After our meal, he continued driving. He planned to drop me off in Skidway, but when he learned I had to go ten or more miles to my destination, he decided to drive me all the way. I mildly protested, but he insisted. This driver, who had no clue who I was, bought me a meal and then dr[...] twenty to thirty miles out of his way to [...]re I didn't have to walk in the free[...]d. It was one of the nicest things so[...] had done for me up until that poin[...]

Later on i[...] life, when John got out of the army, he [...] still amazed at what that driver had done for him. John wanted to repay his kindness in some way, but he didn't know anything about how to contact him. One morning, John decided to stop at a truck stop restaurant in Bridgeport. He asked the waitress working there how many of the men in the dining room were truckers. She laughed and said, "All of them." John told her that he would be paying for all of their breakfasts. She rang him up and he walked out, anonymously. That was his way of thanking that thoughtful trucker.

CHAPTER 5

CHOOSING ROTC OVER GRADUATING ON TIME

In 1964, right before starting his senior year of college, John met an attractive young woman named Esther. He had been single for two years after breaking up with his high school girlfriend. Esther and John were aware of each other and were friendly enough to say "Hi" in passing. But it wasn't until they both attended the wedding of a mutual friend that they really spent any time getting to know one another.

According to John, "Esther was a very outgoing, confident person. She was about medium height, with dark hair, brown eyes, and a great sense of humor." John learned she was going to attend CMU for a degree in education. They hit it off during the wedding weekend, and before long, decided to become a couple.

Due to his working various jobs, John had just one day off each week and that was on Mondays. During the summer, he would work at the store in Skidway on the weekend, and then on Sunday night, he would hitchhike back to Mount Pleasant to see Esther. They would spend the entire day Monday together. He would then hitchhike back to Skidway Monday night to work at the store on Tuesday.

After serving two ROTC training years, a college student had the choice to continue on to advanced ROTC if he was thinking about joining the military after graduating college. It didn't matter what his major was or if he had health issues that would exclude him from joining the army.

Esther and John were spending as much time as they could together before graduation. However, the year John was set to graduate it was announced that Central Michigan University was opening a pilot training program for ROTC cadets to learn to fly aircraft. The basic requirement was that you had to be an undergraduate student to be accepted. John said, "I wanted to fly, so I deferred applying for graduation for one year. I was only a few classes short of another degree, so I decided to take those classes and spend the necessary extra year at CMU to enable me to participate in the pilot training program."

The frosting on the cake was that John was paid twenty-seven dollars a month as part of this flight training. He learned how to march, to whom he should salute, when to salute, and the basics of being in the military.

John earned his second lieutenant commission and completed fixed-wing flight school in 1965. They did not offer helicopter training at CMU during his training. Helicopter pilot training was added to the ROTC curriculum later.

The main reason John says he signed up for the pilot program was because he had never flown in a plane before and he wanted to try it. There was an unspoken fear that the United States would become more involved in the Vietnam Conflict and that there was a possibility of another draft. John was president of the largest fraternity at CMU, and they had eighty-eight members. Of those eighty-eight, only five of them, including John, decided to sign up for the ROTC pilot program. Another 75 percent of the other members ended up switching their degrees to education in hopes of avoiding the draft. Police officers and firefighters were also among those exempt from a draft, but CMU had no degree offering for those fields.

"While in the ROTC program, I had asked Esther to marry me. Esther was very positive at first, but we didn't pull the trigger at that time. Esther and I soon discovered there was a good chance that I was going to Vietnam, so once again I proposed to her. It was eight months after we started dating. She had set a date for the wedding to be at the beginning of 1965. She ended up postponing that date, so I set a new one that I ultimately ended up canceling. When I got my assignment in August of 1965, I was going to be on active duty by October 12. I told Esther, 'I am going on active duty on October 12, and it won't be long after that I'll be headed to Vietnam. Are we going to get married or not?'" This was not the most romantic way to ask a girl to marry you, but John and Esther got married on September 11, 1965.

"We didn't have a big wedding because we didn't have any money. Esther's father was of Mexican heritage and he was a Baptist minister. He was very strict. [Since] I was Catholic and Esther was Baptist, we compromised and got married at a Methodist church in Mount Pleasant, Michigan.

"Our reception was at Falsetta's Restaurant in a little back room. There were only twenty-two people that attended because that was all that we could afford to invite. I can vividly recall receiving three hundred dollars in wedding gifts. The day after the wedding, we walked down the main street in Mount Pleasant and used the money to pay off our credit card charges."

PART II:
THE "HELICOPTER WAR" YEARS

The Vietnam War was called the "Helicopter War." Helicopters were involved in full suppression assaults, medevacs, reconnaissance, and transporting entertainers. Toni Lazzarini is the author of Highest Traditions: Memories of War. *He was the gunner on over one hundred of John Kulhavi's combat missions. According to Lazzarini, there were seven thousand helicopters used in the Vietnam War, four thousand of which were lost. The death rate for helicopter captains and their crews was three times the casualty rate of other military personnel during that time period.*

CHAPTER 6
ACTIVE MILITARY DUTY

On October 12, 1965, John was sent to Fort Knox. Located in Kentucky, it is one of the largest military bases in the United States. While at Fort Knox, he was trained to be a tank commander, in charge of five M60A1 tanks and live ammunition. John was the only tank commander given the responsibility to handle live ammunition.

John says, "Now that I look back on it, they had us do some ridiculous things. I remember that they would call me to go to the garage where the equipment was held. I would have to notify the rest of the team. We had to go to the garage, start up the tanks, and surround a gold vault. They would time us on how fast we could get there. At the time, I thought it was pretty big stuff. I don't even think there was gold in that vault.

"During my time at Fort Knox, Esther was living with some relatives of mine while teaching at a school in Warren, Michigan. We wrote to each other three to four times a week. I loved getting letters from her. It was always great for morale to get a letter from someone, and that goes for any soldier. To know that someone back home cared for you and loved you gave you a compelling reason to keep fighting."

After a year at Fort Knox, John was sent to Fort Wolters for further flight training. Fort Wolters was located four miles east of Mineral Wells, Texas (and it was deactivated as a military base in 1973). "I did basic flight training for six months, and then went on to Fort Rucker [now known as Fort Novosel, a military base in Georgia] for advanced flight training. It was there that I learned how to fly a helicopter." As a side note, singer/songwriter Kris Kristofferson was in flight training on the same base. While there, he wrote the following very funny song about his flight instructor.

"Sky King" by Kris Kristofferson

> *Every mornin' at line you'd see him arrive*
> *He stood five-foot-six, about one-eighty-five*
> *About as broad at the shoulder as he was at the hip*
> *Everybody knew he didn't give a shit, sky king*
>
> *Now some say Sky was born in New Orleans*
> *Where he built himself a rotor on a sewing machine*
> *Cut his teeth on a collective pitch*
> *Old Sky was a low flyin' son of a bitch, Sky King*
>
> *Sky King*
> *Sky King*
> *Short fat sky*

*And then came a day at Stage
　　Field Nine
When his engine failed and men
　　started cryin'
And sirens screamed and hearts
　　beat fast
And everybody thought he'd
　　breathed his last, 'cept Sky*

*Well he pushed that collective on
　　down through the floor
But the damn rotor blade
　　wouldn't turn anymore
So his butt puckered up and with
　　a frightening sound
He just sucked that old chopper
　　up off of the ground, Sky King*

*The ship wasn't hurt but it took
　　half the class
To get the seat cover out of Sky
　　King's ass, Sky King*

*Well they never reopened that
　　landing strip
They just put a marble stand on
　　top of it*

> *And these few words are written*
> *on that thing*
> *Ain't a butt that can pucker like*
> *old Sky King's*

"The helicopter that I would fly in Vietnam was the Bell UH-1 helicopter, known as the Huey, which could fly at low altitudes and speeds, and land in small spaces. The Huey was used by US forces to transport troops, supplies, and equipment, aid ground troops with firepower, and evacuate wounded or killed soldiers. I learned about throttle rotation, how to land a helicopter, survival instincts, and how to win and survive in a flight war.

"In November of 1966, I graduated first in my class from flight school, achieving what I had been anticipating since beginning at Fort Knox."

The United States government was keeping tabs on the environment of Vietnam, aiding where it could, sending troops in to report on the current condition, and occasionally attacking with torpedoes and bombs. US engagement stepped up significantly after President Lyndon Johnson generated increasing public support for the war by March of 1965. By June, the United States had over 82,000 troops deployed in Vietnam.

During that increased-troop-engagement time frame, John and the other ROTC cadets knew they were most likely heading to Vietnam. It was just a matter of time before things would become more intense. By the end of 1965, military leaders were asking for 175,000 more troops to fight the North Vietnamese. Countries that were aiding the South Vietnamese in the conflict were South Korea, Thailand, Australia, and New Zealand.

As the war escalated in Vietnam, the military leaders realized it was a *flight war*. What the United States government learned was that jungle warfare was something our troops were not prepared for, and this gave a tremendous advantage to the North Vietnamese. Thus, the flight-war mentality developed. With John's training as an ROTC cadet and a graduate of the aviation program, he was set to start combat flight school.

He was notified of his deployment to Vietnam in January of 1967.

CHAPTER 7
DEPLOYMENT TO VIETNAM

After a troop was given their deployment date, they were granted a leave to visit their family. This leave was usually for a week or two. However, John was given different plans. His brother, Donald, was also in the army. Due to this fact, the military wouldn't allow them both to be stationed in Vietnam at the same time. John had to wait for Donald to come back to the country before he could be deployed. This did allow John three months to receive extra flight training, and he was allowed to see his family for a few weeks. He chose to spend his time with his mother and Esther, and when he wasn't back in Michigan, he was flying. Because of this delay, John benefited from receiving one hundred more hours of flight training than the rest of his classmates. The skills gained from those extra hours would help a lot later on.

"I have always prided myself on being an overly optimistic person. I don't remember being extremely nervous or anxious in the three months before being deployed. But, I realize now, I was probably a little apprehensive, like anyone would be going into a war zone. I knew it was going to be dangerous, but I also knew I had made a commitment, and that was what I was going to stick to. There were two conflicting assumptions I had made: one part of me thought, 'I will probably be killed over there;' the other part was telling me, 'You're going to come back and be somebody.' I wasn't sure which one was more prominent in my mind: death or hero. But I'm an optimist, and I focused on a hero mentality."

"Gonna Be Somebody Someday" by Dr. Don Steele, Dennis Knutson, and Jerry Taylor

Gonna have me an office in a high rise building
Gonna drive me a Mercedes Benz
Gonna hire me a good lookin' secretary
Gonna have a lot of money to spend

Gonna have me a house on a big ol' hill
Overlookin' all the Puget Sound
From the deck of my yacht I'm gonna take in a lot
A lot of pretty sights as I've been makin' the rounds

I'm gonna be somebody someday
Folks are gonna listen to what I gotta say
No, it's not gonna be like it is today
I'm gonna be somebody someday, someday
I'm gonna be somebody someday

I'm gonna be somebody someday

*Folks are gonna listen to what I
   gotta say
No, it's not gonna be like it is
   today
I'm gonna be somebody someday,
   someday
I'm gonna be somebody someday*

The peak of the Vietnam War was from 1967 to 1968. The United States was approaching 500,000 stationed troops to help aid the South Vietnamese during this time.

In January of 1967, John left Detroit Metro Airport to fly to San Francisco, and from there he caught his flight to Vietnam. All of John's family was there when he was going through security at the Detroit airport. When John looked back, he saw all of them sobbing. He turned around and thought, "'Why are they all crying?' That was when I knew that I couldn't allow my family to believe I was going across the world to die. To keep my word, I needed to believe I was going to live. I decided at that moment that I would come back as a hero or die trying."

John's brother, Donald, left Vietnam the same day John was flying in. One brother's tour in Vietnam was ending as the other's was just beginning.

It was time for John to buckle up his boots. He was headed to Vietnam.

CHAPTER 8
STARTING OFF IN 'NAM: LITTLE BEARS OR BUST

John's flight arrived in Vietnam in the middle of the night. Vietnam is a hot and humid jungle. After getting off the plane, he boarded a bus that took him to the base. He noticed there were screens on the bus windows. They were used to keep the civilians and Viet Cong from throwing grenades through the windows. "Viet Cong" is a term tagged by Ngo Dinh Diem, the former president of South Vietnam, as a derisive name for Vietnamese Communists who engaged in guerrilla warfare on behalf of the North Vietnamese.

In the distance John could see flashing lights and hear the faint sound of artillery going off. All he thought was, "'What have I got myself into?' My emotional state could be described as angst." Angst is defined in the dictionary as a feeling of deep anxiety or dread, typically an unfocused one about the human condition or the state of the world in general.

John had asked to go to Little Bears, the home base of the Twenty-Fifth Infantry Division, located in Cu Chi (pronounced "coo-chee"), Vietnam. Little Bears was made up of an elite group of ranking officers and pilots.

To John's surprise, the Little Bears' brass didn't accept just any pilot. The team there was very particular about who they picked to join them. However, John had heard from others that it was the best unit to be in and contained the best pilots. John believed he was in good shape to be accepted into the Little Bears' helicopter team because of his extra one hundred hours of flight training.

John says, "I really wanted to get into Little Bears. I thought it would be easy. When I arrived on base, they told me I had to do an interview to get in. I couldn't believe I had to interview to get to fight in a war. After the interview, they said, 'If you cut it, you stay, and if you don't, we get rid of you. You're now in a trial period.' I had made it through the first step."

In his trial period, John had to report to one of the five platoon areas. One of his instructors from his advanced flight class was also deployed to Little Bears as one of the platoon leaders. He came up to John and said, "I remember you, hotshot, you're coming with me." They were flying combat and John remembers that the instructor was extremely cocky. John tried to be more humble. Instead of bragging, he wanted his flight skills to speak for themselves. But after a day of flying with him, John realized that in order to make it through the trial period and earn his and the other men's respect, he needed to act just as cocky as the rest of them.

John was not a smoker in high school or college, but he would have a cigarette once in a great while. Almost all of the men that served, including John, started smoking cigarettes in Vietnam. They were flying three to four nights a week and it was a struggle to stay awake. John remembers, "I decided to start a smoking habit because the very strong Camel cigarettes made me cough and choke. This would help me stay awake and helped keep my mind off being away from home. Back then, there were ashtrays built into the cockpit of our Huey. That would never happen today.

"Something that kept me going were the atrocities I had witnessed. Like so many other vets, I rarely talk about the bad things I witnessed in the Vietnam War, but I remember saying to myself early on, when I first got deployed, 'I've got nothing against these people—why am I here?'"

Then something changed that helped John discover his *why*. "When we landed troops at Viet Cong Village, I was aghast at what I saw. I don't know if they did what I witnessed to all kids, but they had cut the arms and legs off a number of children. We saw their bodies as they lay there bleeding to death. There was nothing we could do. That was the Viet Cong's way of telling everyone, 'The next time we come, you give us what we want!' The Viet Cong thrived on intimidation. In that moment, I changed my mind, I found my *why*. I thought, 'If I can stop this, I do know why I am fighting here in Vietnam.'"

While in Vietnam, John flew over three hundred combat missions for the United States Army. At that time, the Air Force was a part of the Army. Today, it is a separate arm of the military. Of these missions and the events that unfolded in Vietnam, he discusses a few missions and conflicts that occurred between January 1967 and January 1968.

The next several chapters describe events from the Vietnam War experienced by First Lieutenant John Kulhavi, call sign Little Bears Three Alpha.

CHAPTER 9
GET OUT OF THE FUCKING PLANE!

John Kulhavi was part of the A Company, Twenty-Fifth Aviation Battalion. He piloted the Huey helicopter. It was a turbine-driven, high-powered helicopter with 750 horsepower. The slicks (the nickname for the transport version of the Huey) that John flew had two post-mounted M-60 machine guns, one on each side, that could pivot in all directions with front and rear stops so an anxious gunner would not accidentally shoot down his own ship.

John's crew consisted of himself (the aircraft commander), the co-pilot, the crew chief, and the gunner. John was the most experienced officer, but the co-pilot monitored the array of gauges and kept John informed of changes. He also took over flight controls if John became disabled. The crew chief performed all the daily maintenance on the ship, and acted as the door gunner on one side of the ship. John's Huey was known as the Little Bear 628. John and other Huey pilots and their crews had a variety of missions, such as courier, mail runs, leaflet drops, counter-mortar, medevacs, and transportation. Suppression missions were the most exhilarating.

The area in which John was located was Cu Chi. That was the main area of combat operations, and contained an estimated ten thousand Viet Cong (the guerrilla fighters that served North Vietnam). The entire area of combat operations was fairly flat, covered with trees, jungle, marshes, and green and brown rice paddies.

"Full suppression mission" was a term that meant the Huey would be going in and firing their machine guns at anything that held the enemy. All John could do was hang on to the flight controls in front of a fairly visible cockpit, and fly the Huey. When taking off, John would put the nose of the Huey in a tilted-down attitude in order to develop lift. This made him more vulnerable to enemy fire than the rest of the crew.

John recalls one mission that took place when he had been in Vietnam for about six months:

> On this mission, the soldiers I picked up had captured two Viet Cong soldiers. I had a few American interrogators in the back that were trying to get the two soldiers to spill their secrets. These two men were tight-lipped. All of a sudden, in my headset I hear a command to start lowering the Huey without letting any of the passengers on board get the sense that we were descending. They were trying to trick the Viet Cong soldiers. I started lowering until I was about five to ten feet off the ground. The two guys had no idea of what was going to happen, being blindfolded.
>
> Suddenly, one of the American

interrogators yelled at one of the Viet Cong soldiers he was interrogating, "Get out of the fucking plane!" and he pushed him out of the Huey. The other guy opened up immediately, thinking he was two thousand feet above the ground and that he would be next. He began spilling the beans so much that the interrogators couldn't get him to shut up.

I don't think the other Viet Cong soldier that was pushed out of the plane was injured; he fell about five feet. However, his fellow soldier had no idea what had happened.

Tony Lazzarini, author of the book *Highest Traditions: Memories of War*, was a gunner on over one hundred of John's missions. Tony offered the following memory:

There were some great pilots. The best ones encouraged you to exchange seats with the co-pilot and learn to fly the ship. My first experience as a novice aviator was with a twenty-four-year-old veteran named First Lieutenant John Kulhavi. We were up about two thousand feet, so he had plenty of time to regain control if I became a little overzealous. I don't remember the exact air speed, but I'm sure it was around seventy knots [about eighty miles per hour].

The two main controls on the helicopter are the collective and the cyclic. The collective gives you up and down, and the cyclic controls the lateral direction—left, right, front, rear, or a combination.

I was a helicopter mechanic before becoming a gunner, and was familiar with the flight controls and theory, but this was the first time I had the opportunity to actually fly one of these things. John told me to put my hands on the cyclic, and said, "Just think where you want to go."

I had seen a lot of John Wayne pictures when he was playing the part of a fighter pilot. It was in the day when planes had those stick controls that came up between the pilot's legs. All the guy had to do was steer the stick in the direction he wanted to go, and that's where it went. I felt pretty good holding the flight controls while John was backing me up on his. I was checking the instrument panel, making sure I was at least flying level, when John mentioned that the airspeed was falling off, and I should drop the nose a little. Well, like the good ol' Captain Wayne did in *Lying Leathernecks*, I shoved the stick forward. Down—and I mean *down*—we went. Talk about touchy! One-hundred-mile-an-hour ride down in an elevator. Lieutenant Kulhavi quickly recovered control, then handed the ship back over to me. From then on, I was the most thinking guy who ever flew a helicopter. He must have had a lot of faith, for he continued to let me in the seat whenever there was an opportunity. We would fly numerous missions together, including ones into

Cambodia in an unmarked Huey and no US Army IDs on any of the crew. We trusted each other with our lives.

A few months after I left for home, a friend wrote to tell me that Kulhavi had been shot down, and the crew had casualties. Lieutenant Kulhavi was wounded, but would recover. Today he is Brigadier General John G. Kulhavi, and I am proud to be his friend.

CHAPTER 10
A TRAITOR AMONGST US

In the Vietnam War, it was hard to trust those around you. It was a fact that there were spies and traitors amongst allies. In the war, American soldiers never knew if the South Vietnamese soldiers were really on their side or if it was a North Vietnamese or Viet Cong soldier pretending to be on their side.

The Viet Cong relied on guerrilla warfare. Guerrilla combat in Vietnam often involved surprise attacks such as ambushes and raids, or sabotage of a vulnerable target. The Viet Cong guerrilla warriors were fighting in their homeland and were therefore usually familiar with the terrain and landscape, and they used this to their advantage in their attacks. Many of the Viet Cong soldiers wore black pajamas and helmets during that time.

Some Viet Cong would pretend to be real South Vietnamese citizens, but in reality they were soldiers. Their tactics were to trick those fighting for the South. Not only did they pretend to be citizens, they also hid in the murky waters of the jungle. They used reeds to breathe while hiding under the water, waiting for the right time to attack. The Viet Cong knew they couldn't win a face-to-face artillery combat battle against the United States and other forces, so ambush, terrorizing, and sabotaging was their way of warfare. According to historians, they attacked troops that were in small groups, and retreated to the safety provided by the cover of the jungle. Creedence Clearwater Revival was alluding to this in their song, "Run Through the Jungle."

"Run Through the Jungle" by Creedence Clearwater Revival

Whoa, thought it was a nightmare
Lord it was so true
They told me don't go walking
    slow
The devil's on the loose

Better run through the jungle
Better run through the jungle
Better run through the jungle
Whoa, don't look back to see

Thought I heard a rumblin'
Calling to my name
Two hundred million guns are
    loaded
Satan cries, "Take aim"

Better run through the jungle
Better run through the jungle
Better run through the jungle
Whoa, don't look back to see

Over on the mountain, thunder
    magic spoke
Let the people know my wisdom
Fill the land with smoke

Better run through the jungle
Better run through the jungle
Better run through the jungle
Whoa, don't look back to see

John recounts:

I would be flying American and South Vietnamese soldiers to a combat sight. The American soldiers would have a gun to the South Vietnamese soldiers' heads the entire flight. This was because many times the Viet Cong would infiltrate our base, pretending to be a part of the South's army. They would get on our planes, drop a grenade, and jump out of the Huey. We would be blown up in the sky, while they fell to their death. The Viet Cong didn't mind losing a soldier as long as it resulted in the death of the enemy.

On the other hand, as Americans, we took the death of a soldier seriously. When we were out there fighting, we were fighting for each other.

It was our duty to fight for God, country, and freedom. However, more realistically, we fought for each other. We fought to save the life of the man sitting next to us, so they could have a life after the war. Every troop was family, a brother you needed to protect. We felt the losses hard, and still do.

While in Vietnam, we had a barber who would cut our hair. He would ask questions and we didn't think anything of it. He had been cutting our hair for a few months before we realized he was actually a Viet Cong spy. He was cutting our hair during the day while attacking during the night. We found out that he was making notes about where our artillery was, how many soldiers we had on base, and more. We had little understanding of the Viet Cong's ability to infiltrate our bases and we underestimated how good they were with guerrilla warfare tactics.

While the US government was saying that we were not expanding the war into Cambodia, this was not true. As you will see, John Kulhavi and his crew were conducting secret missions into Cambodia.

CHAPTER 11
AMMO TO CAMBODIA

The full suppression missions John was given throughout his time serving in Vietnam were of the kill-or-be-killed nature. John says, "The first thing that comes to mind, with respect to the suppression missions, is everything is hurry up and wait. I always wanted to go out and win some conflict. I would ask myself, 'When's the next task?' because I didn't want to wait around. I kept thinking, 'I'm ready!'

"I was also keenly aware that the young men that were a part of my crew would be truly upset if I didn't take them on what we call a full suppression mission with guns blazing in and guns blazing out. They would not be happy if they missed out on the action. They loved the fight and I loved them for that. I honored their bravery and their commitment to never leave a fellow soldier behind. I had all the confidence in my platoon."

Shortly after discovering the traitor on their base, John was given the task of flying ammo to their infantry on the Cambodian border. Ironically, President Johnson was saying that the United States was not engaged on the Cambodian border. Cambodia was supposed to be neutral territory and the American troops were not allowed on the land. This was clearly not true. The battalion commander had asked for volunteers to resupply the soldiers.

John remembers, "There was a terrible monsoon storm happening at this time. To quote the commander, 'Kulhavi, you're leading the flight.' So much for volunteering. He had already picked me to lead the mission. I gathered two other crews to join our effort and I was given the mission plans."

Tony Lazzarini remembers, "Captain

Kulhavi, now promoted, approached me one day to say he would be going on a one-ship mission. This would be a little different from the rest, and he wanted to hand-pick his crew. For the crew chief, he had requested Dave Budde. Dave and I flew together occasionally, and shared the same hooch. [During the Korean War and Vietnam War, hooch was slang for a thatched hut or improvised living space.] For the gunner, John had volunteered me. The only thing that he mentioned was to leave all personal IDs, dog tags, wallet, or anything with the US insignia on it at base. We picked up an unmarked black Huey somewhere in the boonies. We ended up doing several of these missions.

"Once, I asked John the question, 'Did you choose me because you liked me or because you didn't like me?'"

In interviewing John, I asked him to answer that question now. He responded, "I always picked the best soldiers I could for the most dangerous missions. I had the greatest respect for Tony Lazzarini as a gunner and as a person. He was always my first choice, and he joined me on over one hundred missions. He was one of the main reasons why both of us survived Vietnam."

Before they took off on their Cambodian mission to re-supply the troops, John recalls that the commander said, "I want you guys to know, I'm going to be monitoring the radio the entire time you are gone." John thought to himself, "With all due respect, how exactly is that going to help me? Moral support? Me and my guys getting our asses shot off, we're probably going to crash and die near the mountains—fuck the radio and the commander. We had a job to do!

"After I convinced the two other crews to join, we loaded up with ammo. We went to where we thought the area was, which was in between two small mountains. We had to fly between the mountains, land, unload, give them the ammo, and then leave. The weather was so bad, we could hardly see where we were going. In the meantime, we had a ground commander. The ground commander's role was to command and control. The aircraft commander picked up a helicopter that he thought was me and was giving him directions on where to land. He was communicating with the wrong aircraft

—I wasn't even near there. He kept instructing them to continue their approach and we ended up taking the roof off of a hooch with our skids. We almost crashed. We continued to fly with the whole roof of the hooch hanging onto the skids. We ended up finding the infantry men and landed. We then unloaded the ammo and made it back safely."

But there was more to come.

CHAPTER 12
DO OR DIE

John's base had twenty-five Hueys in A Company, the Twenty-Fifth Aviation Battalion, Twenty-Fifth Infantry Division. It was the only aviation unit that was integral to the Infantry Division.

John was asked to take on a new mission. He agreed and was given the mission plans by the unit commander. John shares, "I learned that two Hueys went in only to be met with heavy fire and had to come back to base, accomplishing nothing. There was a third Huey that went in and I could see that it had been shot down. The smoke from the crash told me that it had probably crashed right in our preferred landing zone. I kept my unyielding optimism in the forefront of my thinking—affirming that I was going to come back a hero. But I felt fear creep up my spine as we loaded up the ammo and got situated in the Huey."

John continues, "After noticing the third Huey had crashed into our potential landing zone, I asked the captain, 'What kind of approach were they all taking?' He informed me they were doing a high overhead."

High overhead is a maneuver where the Hueys come in at two thousand feet (but can be higher or lower). Basically, you roll the throttle and then you fall out of the sky and as that is happening, you re-engage the throttle at about fifty feet from the ground and then you land.

John told the captain he was going to try something different because several Huey crews had tried the two-thousand-foot approach and failed, so John was going to do a low-level entry just above the trees. Why? Because a Huey can be very deceptive to the enemy. The enemy can hear it coming from miles away but they can't tell from which direction it's coming because the blades are breaking the sound barrier.

John loved low flying because, by the time the enemy realized they were there, John would be on top of them and then quickly gone. They had only a split second to react.

> The Hueys we flew were D-models. They were underpowered compared to the newer H-models that I flew later. My D-model had 650 horsepower that we upgraded to 750 horsepower. The H-models had 1400 horsepower—a huge wartime advantage. This lack of horsepower determined how I would maneuver the Huey.
>
> I flew at a low level toward the smoke. I could see that the Viet Cong had two bunkers set up with a field between them. If our guys tried to walk into the open field, they would be trapped in a cross-fire. I had not been informed about the bunkers. I had to fly between them to land on the edge of the field.
>
> I don't remember taking any hits

going in. Our troops wouldn't get up and come out of the woods for fear of getting picked off by enemy fire. The troops had no ammo, so my crew chief and my gunner, Tony Lazzarini, put aside their M-60s and began throwing ammo to the troops below as I hovered right to the edge of the woodline. The troops we had been delivering the ammo to quickly grabbed it.

With the Huey model I was flying, I couldn't pick the aircraft straight up; I had to go forward, gain airspeed, and then climb out. The trees were too high, from where I was, to try to get over them, so I had to do a pedal turn and fly back between those two bunkers to get up, where the enemy would be waiting.

I was flying between the two bunkers when I started hearing machine gun fire. We took fourteen hits, and as we were flying back to base, I thought nothing critical was affected.

I went to report back to my captain that we had successfully delivered the ammo to the troops and that they were good to go. He was pleased, to say the least.

After the report, I went back out to the Huey and counted the bullet holes in the aircraft. I discovered that our enemy had poor aim, probably due to not firing into our flight path. Most of their hits were in the back of the cargo compartment and in the tail boom. We got lucky with their poor aim because anything in the middle or front of the aircraft could have led to a different, and probably fatal, outcome.

Insert Huey picture(s)

CHAPTER 13
BACK TO CAMBODIA

The next mission John recounts as one of the most satisfying missions he ever got to fly. This took place about one month after resupplying the American troops on the Cambodian border. Although there were many missions in between these two, this is one that stuck with him throughout the years:

> I was a flight leader and I heard someone come in and wake me up. It was still dark, and I looked at the watch I had been given and saw it was only 3:00 a.m. Usually we didn't

get up and fly until about 5:30 a.m. so I knew this was important. I was given orders to take off my US Army gear, cover up the serial numbers of our Hueys, and take off our US Army badges. I was pretty shocked and thought, "Everyone will know it's an American Huey, with or without the serial number, and why did we care?" The US wasn't into guerrilla warfare like the Viet Cong, but like any good soldier, I didn't question the judgment of my superiors. We would know what they wanted us to know when the time was right.

Soon after we painted over the serial numbers and removed all United States insignia from our flight suits, we found out that it was because we had to go back to Cambodia. The United States had agreed to stay out of Cambodia, which is why we had to go in disguised. If we were caught or were shot down, the army and government could deny our involvement. I don't resent anyone for what they made us do. Once I found out why they got me out of bed at three in the morning to paint an aircraft, I realized it was going to be one of the most important moments in my entire life.

We were informed some time later that the Viet Cong had captured some of our troops and held them hostage in Cambodia. We never leave a soldier behind, and all of us took that motto very seriously. We were given orders to attack at 8 a.m. We surrounded the village with five flights of ten Hueys each. Once we landed, we were able to have soldiers jumping out of the Hueys with all helicopter machine guns pointed forward.

As a flight leader, I was to stay in the Huey so when the mission was accomplished, we could fly out of there as fast as we could. The soldiers ran into the village, and I couldn't see anything; I could only hear sporadic firing.

As I pointed out earlier, Cambodia was officially a neutral country.

We were not supposed to be there. The commander who scheduled the operation was a colonel. He engaged and directed the whole mission. When General Abrams heard about this, he relieved the colonel of his command and sent him back to the United States. Later, President Nixon decorated him in a private session.

All of a sudden, I look up and see five American soldiers running toward my aircraft in black pajamas. While rescuing the American soldiers the Viet Cong took hostage, I noticed that as the soldiers came running out, some were pointing to the water sitting in front of our Hueys. I could see many reeds sticking out of the water in front of us, indicating that the Viet Cong was planning a guerrilla attack. They would hide under water using the reeds as breathing tubes. As soon as they could, my guys pulled grenades and threw them into the water as they boarded the Huey to leave. Only after reflecting on that moment did I realize my helicopter had been a sitting duck. The Viet Cong could have attacked at any moment and I only had a .45 Automatic to protect me.

John mentioned countless times that this was one of his favorite missions. He was able to fully live up to his motto of "Never leave a soldier behind." "We were able to get all of our soldiers held hostage out of Cambodia with no casualties. The difference between us and the North Vietnamese and Viet Cong was that we were willing to risk hundreds of guys on that one mission to save five guys. My philosophy is, 'How can you go on a mission or patrol knowing if you were captured no one would attempt to save you?' If even one soldier had called and said he was captured, our base would still figure out a way to save him."

Relationships, in general, are tricky. Why? Because most of us have a "me-first" attitude. When I put "me" first in a relationship, we lose. So, what can we do? The answer is simple: submit to one another. If we do this, we win.

The Greek military term *hupotasso* laid the groundwork for the "No man left behind" mantra for the US military. *Hupo* means under, and *tasso* means rank. Simply stated, the word *hupotasso* means to rank yourself under—or rank yourself in a way that you are ready to fight for the other. To value others above ourselves requires us to release our "me-first" approach to life: relationships over rights; serving over demanding; and sacrifice over selfishness.

John's Cambodian mission to save otherwise-doomed soldiers can serve as a perfect example of *hupotasso*. Before he would leave Vietnam, he would be on the receiving end of "No soldier left behind."

CHAPTER 14
CRATER MISSION CRASH LANDING

One month before leaving Vietnam, John had to lead his team into what could have been a devastating result. John's unit had lost eighteen of twenty-five Hueys in two days. They were fully aware of the danger but, once again, they were on a mission.

John explains that, early one morning, "as I was getting ready to lift off for my new assignment, a Vietnamese sergeant asked if he could hitch a ride to hook up with his unit where we were going. I agreed, so he climbed on top of the ammo crates.

"As I started my approach, the gearbox that controls the tail rotor was hit by enemy fire from an M55 Quad (which is four machine guns that were used against enemy aircraft like our Huey). The function of the tail rotor is to keep the aircraft from spinning. One round of enemy fire removed that gearbox from my Huey. I was stuck trying to keep my aircraft from spinning out of control and the center of balance was gone. I rolled the throttle off to kill the torque to the engine and it worked—sort of! Instead of spinning, we went nose down into a crater. I remember sitting back in my seat as calm as could be. I keyed the mic and said, 'Oh shit!'"

As the helicopter was descending quickly, John tried to remain calm and collected while realizing the Huey was destined to crash, no matter what he did. He was going through scenarios on the best way to survive the crash without causing injury or, even worse, death to his fellow crew members.

John knew that they would come under more fire. His crew was armed but John questioned whether they would be able to defend themselves against enemy fire. He (the pilot), the aircraft commander, and the rest of the crew were all armed with either a .45 caliber or a .38 caliber pistol, neither of which would be very effective under attack. There were two wells located behind the pilots that housed the gunner and the crew chief. They were armed with M16 rifles that could fire one round or automatic (multiple rounds). These M16 rifles are typically hung on the back of the pilot's and aircraft commander's seats during a flight.

Once a Huey crashes, the pilot and aircraft commander should grab the M16s from the back of their seats. The gunner and the crew chief would arm themselves with the

M60 machine guns that could fire up to two thousand rounds per minute. These machine guns were located on the sides of the Huey.

John describes what happened next:

> I decided to land the Huey right down the side of a thirty-two-foot-deep B-52 bomb crater, the results of an earlier raid. We hit so hard that we tore the skids off the Huey, and the transmission shifted forward, which crushed the top of the pilot's compartment. Until that day, I had always wished I was a little taller. Both of my brothers are close to six feet tall. Had I been their height, I would have been easily decapitated. I never thought to complain about being short after that day.
>
> I don't have any idea of how it happened, but when the aircraft slammed to a stop, I immediately felt the twin fears a pilot has in a circumstance like this: the fear of burning and the fear of being captured. Our Huey was made of aluminum and

magnesium, both of which are flammable. I wasn't worried about the fuel igniting because we didn't use gasoline, which is highly flammable. We used Jet A, which is basically fuel oil but with a much lower flame point. The crew and me being captured by the North Vietnamese or Viet Cong posed more of a threat than the aircraft bursting into flames.

To this day, I don't know whether I climbed out of the aircraft where the windshield had been or if I exited through the top. All I remember is that when I was fully alert, I started scaling the crater wall. I could hear the shooting going on over me. As it turned out, North Vietnamese regulars were on one side of the crater and South Vietnamese with Army Rangers were on the other side. These guys were shooting at each other and we were below in the crater between them.

While I had a sun visor as part of my helmet, I never chose to use it because it was scratched. I always wore my sunglasses. They were much more comfortable and allowed for me to have much better visibility. I remember taking my sunglasses off and throwing them. My face was numb and I didn't know why that was. I also had a pain in my neck, my clothes were ripped up, and I could see other cuts and bruises forming on my skin. I didn't know how any of that happened.

I started scaling the wall without even thinking that there were other people in the Huey. My adrenaline was pumping and I knew it was a bad situation. I got halfway up the crater before I started hearing somebody screaming. I looked back and I saw that it was my crew chief who had his leg pinned under the aircraft.

We hit so hard when we landed that the gunner, who was on the left side of the aircraft, had his harness break loose and he flew across the inside of the cargo compartment and hit the gun mount for the crew chief's M60. His arm was broken in five places. He still had the handles from his M60 in his hand and he couldn't release them. He ran up to me and said, "Lieutenant, Lieutenant! What should I do?" I said, "Grab any weapons you can find," as I was trying to pull the guy out who was pinned under the runners on our crashed Huey. He was screaming like crazy. I couldn't free him. So we went down to grab the M60s. The handguns were not going to do a lot of good. My crew took one M60 machine gun because it had a quick release to that model. The other M60 machine gun had been destroyed. They also added an extra load of ammo.

Until that day, I had no confidence in the South Vietnamese and I can tell you many reasons why. For example, if we were in a firefight and we were landing where the bad guys were (which happened frequently), oftentimes they would refuse to get out of the ship. And we knew that if we took them back to base, they would be executed. So as soon as the ones who would voluntarily jump off the ship jumped, the gunner would grab the other ones and just throw them out. We had to do this.

Knowing all of this, I was surprised when five of these guys left their positions and scaled down the crater. We didn't speak each other's language. Our guys were lying on the ground shooting at the bad guys. And the six of us were pulling this guy out. He was screaming bloody murder.

We could hear the sergeant yelling, "Get away from the son of a bitch, it's going to blow up." That happened when he could see that the fuel line to the engine compartment had broken and flooded the engine compartment with fuel. It was burning and smoke was rolling out of the engine compartment. The sergeant thought it was sure to blow up. Then he yelled something in Vietnamese. As soon as he did that, the five guys that were helping me turned around and took off, making their way back up the side of the crater.

I stayed down in the crater and yelled, "Hey!" They looked back at me and I waved to them to come back. I have no idea why they did what they did, but they came back. I motioned to them to push against the side of the Huey because it wasn't that heavy, and with them pushing it would release the pressure on the leg of my trapped soldier. One of the Vietnamese guys joined me in grabbing the trapped American under the arms and pulling him out from under the aircraft. He was dragged into the woods.

The pilot's name was Tommy Richardson (I was serving as the aircraft commander on this mission). He is retired now and lives in Alaska. He did two tours in Vietnam. At the crash site, I thought he was dead. He was slumped over the controls and his face was covered with blood.

In the meantime, the sergeant

came down into the crater. He was standing there looking at my Huey, and said, "It's amazing what adrenaline does for you." I weighed 143 pounds at the time. I reached out, unbuckled Tommy, and lifted him out of his seat. The same Vietnamese guys that took the crew chief into the woods came back and grabbed him.

Here's an ironic thing: Tommy Richardson was the only guy in our unit that I know of that wore a wedding band. You weren't supposed to wear rings, because cargo hooks were all over the aircraft, and they were afraid that if you caught your ring on the cargo hook and jumped off, you may lose a finger. In his defense, he said the ring was too tight to come off, but while the South Vietnamese carried him off into the woods, they got his ring and his watch off. I guess they figured that was their reward for saving him.

A commander took me to where my guys were. They were all laying there, totally helpless. One guy was screaming and another was covered with blood.

I wanted to give morphine to all of my wounded brothers. We learned in flight school that before you flew every day, the aircraft commander had to sign for two things: one was called an SOI, which stands for Signal Operating Systems. An SOI is a packet that consists of unit nomenclature, the name of the military unit on the ground, and what unit the crew is a part of and their radio frequency (so we could contact them if we had to land in order to pick up the wounded or dead, resupply, or whatever). The other packages contain morphine and pills. My SOI and morphine packet were missing after the crash so I couldn't help.

I also didn't have a weapon. My .45 had flown out of my shoulder holster and crashed through the windshield. It was later found several feet from the Huey—that's how hard we hit when we crashed into the crater. A while later, I knew I needed to get these guys some help, so I went back down into the crater. I climbed into the back of the car compartment and I found pieces of my SOI—and I found the morphine packet.

We wore what we called a "chicken plate," a chest protector that would stop a .30 caliber. There was a velcro pocket in the front and that's where we kept our SOI and our morphine packet. Mine had come out during our landing.

I climbed out of the crater again and went back to where my guys were. One guy was screaming and, little did I know, he had a broken collar bone and some broken ribs. He also had a big chunk of flesh torn out of his leg. This is the same guy we were pulling out from beneath our Huey.

I gave him the injection of morphine and bent the needle in his collar so that the medevac would know how much morphine he had taken. After the first injection, he kept on screaming. I decided he needed another injection, and that did it—he passed out. I was glad the second injection worked because I knew that a third injection would kill him.

I then went to check on Tommy. "Tommy, how do you feel?" His face was covered with blood. You cannot believe how much blood. I could not put a tourniquet on his neck, so there was nothing I could do. Tommy opened up his eyes and said, "Jesus Christ, John, do I have a headache." His eyes were as big as saucers and then he passed out. It ended up being a good thing because, when you pass out, your blood pressure drops. I grabbed branches and leaves, anything I could find, to cover his body to keep him as warm as possible.

I'm here in the woods with three other guys. The Vietnamese soldiers are gone, the advisor's gone, and I picture myself like Davy Crockett or Jim Bowie at the Alamo. I've got an M60 and two bandoliers of ammo. I could start blazing away until I ran out of ammo and then it would be all over. That's all I could do. I had three incapacitated guys and I had nowhere to go.

Someone, probably the sergeant, called for a medevac ship. It had come about thirty minutes after we went down and left because they came under fire. It looked like we were there for the night, but about twenty minutes later, the medevac team returned. This time, they were not shot at, but they had no place to land. So they hovered over the crater as close to the edge as they could get. Two medics, a crew chief, and I dragged these injured guys to the medevac H-model Huey. Thank God for our commitment to "No man left behind." This time, I was the beneficiary.

Not always were soldiers as lucky as John and his crew. Tony Lazzarini recalls his experience as a gunner assisting medevac missions assessing crews that did not survive. He says, "The reality of war always brought back to me the flights to the morgue at Tan Son Nhut [Air Base], loaded with body bags, precious cargo entombed in a leather fabric. We flew these at night under a cover of darkness. Appropriate, now that I recall, a dark lone ship delivering sadness. At the landing pad, they could be hustled off into a gray Quonset hut to be prepared for a long journey home. They were the sons, fathers, or brothers deprived from living the guarantee of life, justice, and the pursuit of happiness."

John elaborates further on how he questioned whether all of the men could make it onto the rescue helicopter. He says, "I had never seen an H-model Huey before. I had been flying the D-model. We got our three injured guys into the medevac Huey. I told the aircraft commander, 'You're going to be overloaded, so leave me here. Come back to get me when you can. You're never going to get all of us on.' He said, 'This is an H-model—hop on board, it'll be fine.' I really wasn't going to argue with the guy: I jumped on, joining two guys up front, three in the back, and four other guys. That is a very heavy load for a Huey. Then, all of a sudden, the pilot took the Huey straight up one hundred feet. I remember thinking, 'Holy shit, I've never seen a Huey fly like this before!'"

The medevac team flew the men to a mosh tent that was set up right on the edge of the battlefield. They came running out with litters and put three of the men on the litters. They had one for John as well, but he said, "No, I'm fine," and walked himself into the tent. A doctor ran up to him and frantically stated, "I need to get you stitched up, you're bleeding pretty badly." John replied, "I'm fine. Just take care of my men."

John remembers, "There was a cot there and I sat watching them operate on my guys. When they were done, the doctor came up to me and commanded, 'I have got to get you stitched up. Stand up!' That's when I realized I couldn't stand up. 'KULHAVI! I said stand up, we need to get you stitched!'

"I couldn't stand up and I didn't know what was wrong. After a while, the doc figured out what had happened: When we hit, I tore all of the muscles in my back. Adrenaline had kept me moving while being stranded, but once I sat down, everything tightened up and the pain finally set in."

The doctor stitched him up and then wrapped his head in gauze. John had received a huge gash on his head, something he also hadn't been aware of due to the adrenaline.

"Sometime after dark, they loaded the four of us on a Huey and flew us back to our base camp at Cu Chi where they had built their hospital. The doctor said to me, 'There is nothing more we can do for you. Do you want to stay at the hospital or go back to your unit?' I said, 'Take me back to my unit.' They put me on a litter and carried me out to a truck. Some guys in my unit were passing us and they saw me on the litter. They went back and told the commander that I had had half of my head blown off. When we reached my hootch, they put me on my bed and I laid there for three days in a fetal position.

"Every day, a doctor would come over to give me injections in my back. I'm sure they were muscle relaxers. My guys would bring me food. They would lift me up with both their arms and we would call them the sixholers. They would carry me up high to and from the bathroom, telling me they wanted to make sure I had no fear of flying. Three days later, within an hour of when I could finally stand, I was back in my flight suit and in the cockpit of the Huey.

"The commanders want you to get right back in the aircraft to start flying again, so you don't think too much about what has happened and give in to a fear of flying. So we just flew around the base and landed. We did this for about an hour and I was good to go."

Tommy Richardson was evacuated to Germany with a severe head injury. He came back to the unit three-and-a-half months later. By the time he came back, John had already rotated back to the States. "I was told later that he flew two more combat missions and went ballistic on both of them because he had had a lot of time to think about what had happened. He finished his first tour supervising maintenance at our maintenance facility.

"Tommy was a really good guy. His son called me about ten years ago. He told me his dad did a second tour in Vietnam. When he left the service, he went to work for the post office. He retired from that job. He then said, 'My dad has been telling me stories about you from the days when we were little kids. He's coming back to the States for a family reunion in some town near Boston. I would like it very much if you could come and see my dad. I know he would love to see you.' I had a conflict and was unable to attend the reunion, so I have not had the chance to talk with Tommy Richardson again."

A chinook was used to raise the Huey a few days after the crash. It was placed in a field at John's base camp. Once he could walk, John went to see it and took some pictures. It was 100 percent destroyed.

John recalls one officer saying, "How many soldiers died on that ship?" and John replied, "No one." The guy said, "How do you know?" and John said, "Because I was the one flying it."

Somebody wrote a caption underneath the picture. It reads, "Who says you can't land a Huey upside down?"

CHAPTER 15
TONY LAZZARINI REMINISCES

When talking about John, Tony says, "John is one of the greatest guys I have met in my seventy-six years. He was always taking care of his guys. In the helicopter, we all depend on each other. Captains depend on GIBs (guys in the back). I was a GIB gunner, grenades, ammo, etc. I could fire five hundred rounds a minute. After each use, I had to break down my weapon and completely clean it. I once asked John if my pulling the trigger and letting the bullets fly made him proud of me. John responded with, 'Yes, but you never had to walk home, did you?'

"One of the greatest things to this day

was when I was able to call John by his first name. He had always been 'Captain' to me. One evening, John called me from the San Francisco airport. We talked until four in the morning, and we chatted about how he taught me to fly the helicopter. We also reminisced on my first flying experience where I ended up putting our helicopter into a nosedive. John very alertly corrected and we were okay. John's advice was, 'Just think where you want to go, and your mind and body will do the rest.'

"I remember we had a pilot form New Jersey. Unfortunately, he is one of the pilots we lost. But pilots have to stay calm. One time he said to me, 'Hey Lazzarini, I'll let you fly the helicopter if you let me shoot the machine gun.' I was flying over the free-fly area, and he let off about one thousand rounds of ammo. Later on, in one of our search-and-destroy missions, we had ten helicopters, each carrying as much ammo as they could carry, one ship flying low as a decoy. We wanted to surprise the enemy but someone unloaded on us. I dropped grenades and the pilot led us on a low-level assault.

"There were eighty guys in ten helicopters, eight in each. We caught them by surprise. Shit was flying all over the place. Suddenly, I heard a .45—the pilot had shot a guy in an enemy helicopter. Apparently, that enemy had not met someone from New Jersey."

I asked Tony if he was ever shot down in the military, and he said, "Five times, but it was all by nurses. I was never shot down in flight."

CHAPTER 16
POST 'NAM

There are a few issues that arise when we think about the Vietnam Conflict, including the treatment of soldiers, the mental and physical post-war effects, and whether our side won or lost.

In January of 1968, John received his orders that he had finished his tour in Vietnam and was being deployed back home. During this time, Vietnam soldiers were still being treated with respect and praised when they got home.

Other soldiers that came home after March of 1968 weren't so lucky. As the rise of technology became prevalent in more American's lives, for the first time ever a war was being televised and photographs were distributed, so Americans saw the horrors of what a war really was. Unfortunately, the soldiers were blamed. Soldiers couldn't wear their uniforms while in the country because many people would spit on them, yell profanities, and much worse. This was never John's experience when he came home but he heard of many soldiers who got treated like this in the following years.

Songwriter Tom Russell does an excellent job of capturing the after-effects of the Vietnam Conflict. The following song, "Veterans Day," is just one of his renderings that moves the emotions of soldiers and of the rest of us.

"Veterans Day" by Tom Russell

> *Well I used to hang out down at the VFW hall*
> *And stare at the photographs up on the wall*
> *Of the neighborhood boys that died*
> *in the wars we've been through*

*And the hand-lettered sign
  that said
remember Jimmy McGrew
Well Jimmy went to 'Nam back
  in 1965
But there's a lot of men here that
  think
Jimmy McGrew's still alive
Though they carved his name
on a stone in Washington DC
His brother said that stone
don't prove a thing to me*

*It's veteran's day and the skies
  are gray
Leave the uniforms home cause
there ain't gonna be a parade
But we'll fill up a glass for
  the ones
that didn't make it through
And leave a light in the window
  tonight
for Jimmy McGrew*

*There's a hot rain fallin'
on the back streets of Saigon*

There's an old soldier stumblin'
*   down the alley*
with his mama-san
Lord his eyes are cloudy
and his arms are black and blue
He's just hangin' by a thread
and he looks like Jimmy McGrew
It's veteran's day and the skies
*   are gray*
Leave the uniforms home cause
there ain't gonna be a parade
But we'll fill up a glass for
*   the ones*
that didn't make it through
And leave a light in the window
*   tonight*
for Jimmy McGrew
And keep it burnin' bright
there may still be a lot of Jimmy
*   McGrews over there*
But we'll fill up a glass for
*   the ones*
that didn't make it through
And leave a light in the window
*   tonight*
for Jimmy McGrew

John says, "During that time, the American citizens blamed the soldiers, but they didn't understand that we didn't have a choice. As regular soldiers, we do not get to pick the battles, where we are stationed, or which conflicts America becomes involved in. That is completely up to the politicians, not the soldiers. We are there to do our job, which is to protect our country."

In the movie *The Messenger*, Woody Harrelson and Ben Foster play the parts of two soldiers tasked with the job of informing next of kin. After filming the movie, Harrelson stated, "I've been an outspoken peace advocate for good reason. But what was missing from my own philosophy was a real understanding of what these soldiers go through. However you feel about the war, I have a lot of respect for these soldiers. I hope this film gives these warriors the light they deserve."

Not only was the treatment of the soldiers horrific upon returning, but drawing from collected data from Vietnam War history, and according to a survey by the Veterans Administration (or VA, which is a government organization that provides assistance to individuals that have served in the armed forces), around five hundred thousand of the three million troops who served in Vietnam suffered from post-traumatic stress disorder (PTSD). Divorces, suicide, alcoholism, homelessness, and drug addiction were markedly higher among Vietnam veterans. The published rates are probably low because many of the soldiers refused to disclose that they suffered from after-war effects.

Vietnam veteran John Prine wrote a powerful song that tells the story of what happened to one vet who was adversely affected by the war, entitled "Sam Stone."

"Sam Stone" by John Prine

> *Sam Stone came home*
> *To his wife and family*
> *After serving in the conflict*
>   *overseas*
> *And the time that he served*
> *Had shattered all his nerves*
> *And left a little shrapnel in his*
>   *knees*

But the morphine eased the pain
And the grass grew round his
*   brain*
And gave him all the confidence
*   he lacked*
With a purple heart and a monkey
*   on his back*
There's a hole in daddy's arm
*   where all the money goes*
Jesus Christ died for nothin' I
*   suppose*
Little pitchers have big ears
Don't stop to count the years
Sweet songs never last too long on
*   broken radios,*
Sam Stone's welcome home
Didn't last too long
He went to work when he'd spent
*   his last dime*
And Sammy took to stealing
When he got that empty feeling
For a hundred dollar habit
*   without overtime*
And the gold rolled through his
*   veins*
Like a thousand railroad trains

And eased his mind in the hours that he chose
While the kids ran around wearin' other peoples' clothes
There's a hole in daddy's arm where all the money goes
Jesus Christ died for nothin' I suppose
Little pitchers have big ears
Don't stop to count the years
Sweet songs never last too long on broken radios,
Sam Stone was alone
When he popped his last balloon
Climbing walls while sitting in a chair
Well, he played his last request
While the room smelled just like death
With an overdose hovering in the air
But life had lost its fun
There was nothing to be done
But trade his house that he bought on the GI bill
For a flag-draped casket on a local hero's hill

There's a hole in daddy's arm
  where all the money goes
Jesus Christ died for nothin' I
  supposed
Little pitchers have big ears
Don't stop to count the years
Sweet songs never last too long on
  broken radios

Not only are there mental and emotional effects, there are also the physical factors such as loss of limbs, blindness, deafness, and other debilitating injuries suffered during the Vietnam Conflict.

For most people, Vietnam and Agent Orange will always be associated in their minds. Agent Orange was a chemical used to eliminate forest coverage in which the North Vietnamese and Viet Cong hid. This was a pesticide, and the United States sprayed more than twenty million gallons on Cambodia, Laos, and Vietnam.

Come to find out later, this caused cancer, birth defects, rashes, and severe psychological and neurological problems, not only to the people of these countries, but also to our own soldiers. There have been various lawsuits over Agent Orange which have allowed the VA to respond and give medical relief to veterans affected by Agent Orange's side effects.

John explains, "I know a lot of troops suffered from PTSD or after-war effects once coming home from Vietnam. I was lucky and didn't have any of these effects. The only thing I remember was, two or three days after I got home from active duty, I was sleeping when a siren went off. I jumped out of bed and hid in the closet. On base, if a siren went off, it meant there was a ground attack and we had to hide in a bunker as quickly as possible. That was the only bad thing that happened when I got home, and I consider myself lucky for that.

"As for the Agent Orange side effects, I never had any side effects that I know of. But I had been flying in planes, not living and sitting in the jungle like the ground soldiers who had to inhale and breathe it all day, everyday. However, I do know President George W. Bush did a lot to improve the VA and get many Vietnam veterans access to adequate healthcare and help."

Now onto a point of great debate: Did

the United States win or lose the Vietnam War? The United States started pulling troops out of the Vietnam War in the spring of 1969. After being in the middle of the conflict for eight years, the US decided to listen to their citizens who were protesting the involvement in the war. Representatives from the United States, North Vietnam, South Vietnam, and the Viet Cong met in Paris to discuss ending the war. They came to a conclusion, and all four parties signed a peace treaty on January 23, 1973. The last American troops departed Vietnam on March 29, 1973. One would think that this would be considered a win for the United States, but that is not where the story ends.

Before the United States completely pulled out of Vietnam, the North Vietnamese and the Viet Cong disregarded the cease-fire and the full-on war resumed. There were many South Vietnamese casualties, but the United States did not become re-involved. This can be taken two ways: While the United States was on the winning side when they were involved in the war, South Vietnam started to lose after their departure. This has led many citizens to believe we lost the war, because in the end, the South Vietnamese lost. However, this soldier's point of view is different.

John says, "The United States did not lose the war. We never lost a major battle, and we were the ones who initiated the peace treaty. It was not the United States' fault that the war began again after the North Vietnamese went back on their word. We won while we were there and initiated talks of peace."

CHAPTER 17
MEETING DIGNITARIES

As John reflects back on his experiences while serving in the war, he feels very fortunate to have had the opportunity to meet many dignitaries. On military bases, entertainment tours were organized and sponsored by the United Service Organizations (USO). Through these tours, John met entertainers like Charlton Heston, James Garner, Martha Ray, and Bob Hope.

John shares, "One of my fondest memories while serving in the war was when I met Charlton Heston, a famous actor at the time. It was quite an interesting story. In our unit, the highest award one could get was the

Distinguished Flying Cross. That award is on par with the Silver Star. To us pilots, it was like getting the Medal of Honor. I feel very fortunate, because I was the only guy in the entire unit that got two."

When Charlton Heston came to John's division headquarters, John had no idea this was taking place because he had flown the entire night and was exhausted. John knew that he had the next morning off, so he went to bed. In the meantime, Heston was at the public information office, and he had asked what was happening on post. The public information officer informed him that there was recently an award ceremony where the Distinguished Flying Cross was awarded to one of the pilots. Heston asked, "Can I meet him?" and they said that he could. They put him in a jeep, along with his aide that was with him. They drove over and parked right in front of John's hooch. John remembers, "Heston came in, and he started shaking my bunk. When I woke up and saw him standing there, I thought I had died and that he was Moses.

"I remember as I sat up, he reached over and shook my hand and said, 'I'm Charlton

Heston.' I responded, 'Pleased to meet you.' I didn't know what the hell to say to him. I said, 'Would you like a beer?' I don't even drink beer. He said, 'Yeah, that sounds good.' In the meantime, I had twenty-five or thirty guys standing outside of my hooch. Everybody wanted to see Charlton Heston. I got up and got dressed. He stood there talking to me the entire time. We had a little living room area that we built in our hooch. One of the guys that was living in the unit had a monthly subscription to *Playboy*. He would take the centerfold out, put it on a piece of cardboard, cover it with a piece of plastic, and display them all around the room. I told all the guys standing outside to come and squeeze in my hooch. The place was jam packed. Heston was sitting down, and I was sitting across from him while everybody else was standing up and watching. I remember asking him for a photo or an autograph. He then asked his aide, 'Will you grab my briefcase out of the jeep?' The aide brought it in and Heston opened it. Joan Collins was the Playmate of the Year in 1965, and she had given Heston an original black-and-white nude photo. She had autographed and addressed it to Charlton Heston. So Heston wrote on it, 'Hell, you don't want my photo,' and he signed it and gave it to me. I still have it to this day.

"When I met Heston, he was as down to earth as can be, and so was James Garner. I picked Garner up, and I remember being asked to fly him to some unit in the middle of nowhere. When we had landed, there was nobody there. We had about twenty minutes just to shoot the breeze before the jeep came over to pick him up. A couple months before that, I was on vacation in Hawaii with Esther, and we went to the movies to see *Grand Prix*. In this movie, he played the part of a Grand Prix race car driver. I said to him, 'Was *Grand Prix* your last movie?' He looked at me and said, 'I hope it isn't.' Those were the kind of answers he gave."

Martha Raye was one of the most interesting stars that John had met. She went on a USO tour and loved the soldiers so much that when the tour ended, she didn't go back to the United States. She was not sponsored by anybody, except herself. She had a backpack, a pair of jungle fatigues, and a low-battery-operated recorder with music.

Whenever there was a group of soldiers together, Martha would put on a show for them. John remembers getting calls about her all the time. "I received a call in the middle of the day when there was a mortar attack on Black Virgin Mountain. She was on top of a mountain and I had to go get her out of there. You never knew where she would be next: trucks, helicopters, just putting on shows."

Bob Hope was another interesting star that John feels very fortunate to have met. Hope would travel to Vietnam every year the war went on. He would typically stay two weeks and would do two shows a night. Hope was never able to stay right in Vietnam when he would visit because he was too big of a security risk.

John shares, "Around the time of one of Bob's visits, we had captured some North Vietnamese documents that revealed to us that they had a reward on him, bigger than they did on General Westmoreland, who was commander of all allied forces of Vietnam. They thought it would have been a great propaganda coup to get Bob Hope. After his second show, they would load him and his troupe on three C-130s [cargo aircrafts] and fly him to Utapao Air Force Base in Thailand. This was much safer than being in Vietnam. The next morning, at an ungodly hour, they would load up and go back to Vietnam. We got an order informing us, for security reasons, that he was going to be at our base camp sometime during the two-week period. They couldn't identify what day or time for security purposes. They said, 'You'll be given two-hours' notice of when he's going to be there and any troops that are on Main Post can go to the show.'

"Now the interesting thing is we had patrols out twenty-four seven to make sure our perimeter was clean with no bad guys. When the three C-130s came to land on final approach, we didn't know which one Bob Hope was, but the bad guys did—the one he was in received fire all the way down to the runway, even though we had patrols out to make sure that didn't happen. Then they took him by jeeps and trucks to a stage that we had built. There was a hill where about one thousand soldiers sat to watch. I never got to see the show, but I could hear it. My job was to park ten Hueys right next to where the stage was. Before the show started, I went up to Bob Hope, Les Brown, Joey Heatherton, or whoever his dignitaries were. I told them, 'If the siren goes off, that means we have either ground attack or mortar attack. We won't have time to load you, your equipment, or your instruments to take you back to the airfield. Leave everything and head for the aircraft that you're assigned to.' I gave each one of them a number. Then I said, 'We will crank those Hueys up quickly, and we'll fly you to Tonistoot Air Force Base, right outside of Spigot.' Fortunately, the siren never went off."

Some of the entertainment provided for the troops was based in humor, e.g. Bob Hope. But it is best not to forget that the soldiers themselves had some great humor, too. For example, Tony Lazzarini, in his book *Highest Traditions: Memories of War*, wrote a fictional letter that a soldier might write to his parents back home. The letter reads:

Hi folks:

Looks like a great day today. Got up early because of a mortar attack. This time they nailed the generators for the hot water showers. At least they did not hit the beer hall. HA HA! Went over to the mess hall for some powdered eggs and recombined milk. Lucky for me, I spotted the cockroach legs deep-fried with the bacon. Might have been something else. They got quite a collection of bugs over here. The locals just pull heads and legs off live ones and pop them in their mouths. I'm down fifteen pounds and don't eat much anyway. Happy to say my foot rot is not getting worse. Found out the annoying itch I have is just crabs and nothing contagious.

 I got the package you sent to help me celebrate my twentieth birthday. The fresh fruit and salami were a big hit with the guys I shared them with. We wired up a couple of fat ones and ate everything in one sitting.

    Must be about 115 outside. We were afraid it might get hot today. Thank God the weather cooled off.

    I had a great time on my R & R to Bangkok. Met this really nice hooker and she showed me around town. Did you know the government regulates them? I tell you, it's the best buy you can get for only twelve bucks a night! Spent the entire week hanging out with her. She's great. Too bad they haven't legalized prostitution in the States. I'm all for it!

    We're getting ready to go out on

a big assault today. We will be packing about one hundred grunts and dropping them off in the Hobo Woods. It's that place I wrote to you about last week where we lost three ships going in. Maybe today I can get me a couple more gooks to make up for it. I'm still behind Sgt. Kellogg for most kills but catching up fast.

Have to make this short 'cause I have to re-arm the Huey with smoke grenades and ammo.

Will write again soon.

Your loving son

PART III:
TRANSITIONING BACK INTO THE STATES

John recalls, "Esther probably saved my life. She asked me, 'Why don't you try civilian life for a year? If you don't like it, you know, you could always go back.' I had been shot down twice, and she was fearful that if I went back, I would get killed. And I probably would have. I thought that was a reasonable request."

CHAPTER 18
THINGS COME IN THREES

John was shot down a second time on December 28, 1967. Because of that, the brass let him come home three days early. Coincidentally, a succession of things happened during the three days after he left: the first was the start of the Tet Offensive, and had he been there, John believes he might have died; the second was the passing of his father; and the third was the conceiving of his daughter, Lisa. We will briefly discuss each of them.

The first was the Tet Offensive. According to *history.com*, by the end of 1967, Hanoi's communist leadership was growing impatient, and sought to strike a decisive blow aimed at forcing the better-supplied United States to give up hopes of success. On January 31, 1968, some seventy thousand Democratic Republic of Vietnam (DRV) forces under General Vo Nguyen Giap launched the Tet Offensive (named for the lunar new year), a coordinated series of fierce attacks on more than one hundred cities and towns in South Vietnam. Taken by surprise, US and South Vietnamese forces nonetheless managed to strike back quickly, and the communists were unable to hold any of the targets for more than a day or two.

Reports of the Tet Offensive stunned the US public, especially after news broke that General Westmoreland had requested an additional two hundred thousand troops, despite repeated assurances that victory in the Vietnam War was imminent. With his approval ratings dropping in an election year, President Johnson called a halt to bombing in much of North Vietnam (though bombings continued in the south) and promised to dedicate the rest of his term to seeking peace rather than re-election.

Johnson's new tack, laid out in a March

1968 speech, was met with an originally positive response from Hanoi, and peace talks between the US and North Vietnam opened in Paris that May. However, as soon as the talks began, they stalled. Despite the later inclusion of the South Vietnamese and the Viet Cong, the dialogue soon reached an impasse, and after a bitter election season marred by violence, Richard M. Nixon won the presidency eight months into the peace talks. At this point, the only thing the two sides had agreed on was the shape of the conference table.

John said, "The Tet Offensive was probably the biggest battle. I would have been on the post base where everybody came for out-processing, where soldiers have no weapons. I could have been there.

"On my return to the United States from Vietnam, I flew to San Francisco. We had to stop to refuel. [The flight] took twenty-seven hours. My crew chief was with me, and he was from Chicago. We rotated together. We went to the airport at San Francisco, and we couldn't get a flight until the next morning. We called Tony Lazzarini. He lives in San

Francisco, so he met us at the airport, and we sat in the bar all night and left the next morning. There was a snowstorm in Detroit, and I was wearing a short-sleeve shirt and khakis. Esther was coming to the airport to pick me up. I had called her from San Francisco and told her what time we would be arriving."

On her way to pick John up, Esther got caught in a traffic jam in the blizzard. She was sitting in her car, crying, when a semi driver walked up and asked her, "What's wrong?" She said, "I am picking up my husband, who is coming back from Vietnam, and I can't get to the airport." The semi-truck driver said, "Get on my back bumper and stay there; I'm gonna take you to the airport." She got to the airport in time.

The second event was the passing of John's father. His brother, Donald, wanted to get married, and he wanted John and their father there. Two days after John arrived home, Esther, his brother Larry, and John all flew to Salt Lake City for the wedding.

"My father had flown out earlier that morning because he wanted to see the city, and we weren't going to make it until later in the afternoon. My brother Donald, his fiancée, and her parents met us at the airport. They wanted to take us all out to dinner. My father said that he had been walking all day and wanted to get a good night's sleep, because it would be a long day tomorrow. I had been on a plane for twenty-seven hours, and I was tired, too. We both passed on going to dinner.

"At about two o'clock in the morning, the phone in my room rang. The guy at the desk said, 'The man below you has the same name as you, and he is sick. You better go see him.' My father was John Kulhavi Jr., and I am John G. Kulhavi. By the time I went to his room, he had passed. We canceled the wedding, flew home, and planned a funeral."

John's brother held the wedding a couple of days later. Nobody was there, because John couldn't get any more leave time and the others couldn't afford airline and hotel tickets. He got married with only his wife's family present. They have been married for over fifty years now.

The third event turned out to be quite a surprise when John and Esther found out that their daughter Lisa had been conceived during that three-day period.

CHAPTER 19
WHERE THERE IS A WILL, I WANT TO BE IN IT

John's father had been telling his children that when he died, they were all going to get rich. "After his death, we were all looking forward to reading his will. My father had been a tool and die maker. Upon returning to Detroit on our flight from Salt Lake City, my stepmother wanted to stop at the shop where my dad had worked and look through his toolbox. He told somebody that all of his valuables were in his toolbox, so we agreed to stop there.

"Surprisingly, she had already gotten an injunction stating that no one but her could get into my father's toolbox. It was clear she was after the money. However, as we were leaving Dad's factory, the owner of the factory called me aside. He whispered, 'Come back here late tonight and I will let you go through your dad's toolbox.' In essence, all we got was a golden globe with a matching cigarette lighter from his previous girlfriend, the one he had left my mother for."

A while later, John and his siblings arranged to go see what was in his dad's safety deposit box at the bank. They found that their stepmother already had her attorney there, along with somebody from the IRS. They brought a safety deposit box out and all it contained was a $10,000 insurance policy, a warranty for a car battery, four $2 bills, an old birthday card from his girlfriend, and an arrowhead John's father had designed for an archery company.

"Somehow my stepmother thought until the day she died that we got to the safety box before she got her injunction," John remembers, "but really there was nothing in it. The next day, we went to her house to go pick out the coffin. My father's first job after high school was embalming for AJ Brando funeral home. We went to the funeral home to pick everything out. We talked to our stepmother ahead of time and I said, 'We don't know who the beneficiary of the insurance policies is. If you're the beneficiary, you pay for the funeral, and if we are, we'll pay for it.' She agreed.

"My father loved his initials on everything. We picked out the most expensive casket they had. I said, 'I want the letters *JK* on top of the casket.' We wanted limos too. He was going to go out in style. The funeral costs were near as much as the policy was worth."

When they went to settle up the bill with Brando, the owner, he told their stepmother, "You're responsible for the costs, because you are the beneficiary." Their stepmother said, "I'm not paying for it, I didn't want all that stuff." Brando said, "I hate to tell you this, but you're responsible for it."

At the time, John had been storing all his life's belongings in his father's attic. "After the funeral, I went to my father's house with my favorite Polish uncle, Eddie. When we got there, my stepmother opened the door, and we walked in and went straight upstairs. I had a box full of stuff, and my uncle had a box full of stuff stored there. My stepmother's son stood in front of the door. He was a tall and skinny kid, and I was in phenomenal shape at the time from Vietnam. I said to the kid, 'You have a choice: I'm going to go around you or I am going to go over you, but I am walking out with my stuff.' He moved over. My uncle slammed him against the wall and said, 'Stay out of it,' and just held him there. And we walked out with our stuff.

"At the time we found out that Esther was pregnant, we had no plans to have children. Nevertheless, it was happening. I had been to war for a whole year. After the baby was conceived, I told Esther that I had been saving up for over a year. I think she thought I was talking about money. Enough said."

After coming back from the war, John was still on active duty, stationed at Fort Wolters Air Force Base in Texas. He was in charge of the academic classes. He spent approximately a year and a half at Fort

Wolters, and it was during this time that his first daughter Lisa was born.

John said, "I was a senior captain by virtue of timing. That means I was promoted before by my contemporaries. I had a phenomenally good record. I got promoted to lieutenant, captain, and major ahead of my contemporaries because I had a better record than they did. I was put in charge because I was the highest ranking captain. While I had twenty-seven captains that worked for me, at the end of the month we all drew the same pay. At that point, I decided it might be a good time to leave the military, so I talked to Esther.

"Esther probably saved my life. She said, 'Why don't you try civilian life for a year? If you don't like it, you know, you could always come back.' I was shot down twice while in Vietnam and she was fearful that if I went back that I would get killed. And I probably would have." John agreed with Esther's reasoning.

"Back in the States, I needed to find a career, and not just any career. I had always found ways to make money, and the financial field seemed to be calling my name.

Would it be a lifetime at General Motors? The automotive industry never really appealed to me. I wanted whatever I found for my future to be based in entrepreneurship. I set my sights on Merrill Lynch, even though I knew nothing about financial investing."

CHAPTER 20
SUCCESS AT MERRILL LYNCH

John decided to find a career that would compensate him based on his own effort and ability. He turned down six different jobs interviewing with General Motors because his assessment of that type of work environment was that promotion and monetary gain were *not* based on effort and ability, but on one simple factor: how many years you lived.

Determined to find a good job to support his now-growing family, John decided to apply for a job in the financial investment industry. He admits he had none of the required credentials and knew nothing about the brokerage industry.

"Merrill Lynch was a very prominent financial advising company. It is still top-shelf. While I had applied at four such institutions, the first to respond to my application was the Detroit office of Merrill Lynch, located in the Fisher Building. At the time, I was working at the primary helicopter training center in Texas.

"Getting a chance to work at Merrill Lynch would be an opportunity I couldn't miss out on. I booked a flight from Texas to Detroit and left for the interview as soon as I could."

That flight ended up being late, and once he finally arrived in Detroit, John didn't even have time to change out of his uniform. He had to go to the interview in what he was wearing, and he made it to the appointment just in time. To this day, John believes that wearing the uniform is what got him that job.

"I didn't have a background in financial advising; I was a psychology major turned ROTC cadet turned brigadier general. What did I know about the financial advising world? Basically nothing. In spite of all of that, I was determined to get the job.

"Fred Picker, the manager who interviewed me, had a military background and knew what the awards on my uniform meant. He was impressed by them. Fred administered two tests: one was an aptitude test and the other was an IQ test. Once I passed, I think it gave Fred all the information he needed to know that I had the aptitude and intelligence to get the job done."

After his interview, John flew back to Texas and a few days later received a call from Fred. He wanted John to come to Detroit and meet him for lunch. John booked yet another plane ticket and arrived for what he hoped was an official job offer. "At lunch, Fred and I talked more about who I was and my tour in Vietnam. Fred then informed me that the company wanted me back to complete one or two more interviews. I looked at Fred and said, 'We have had two personal meetings; you know everything about me that I could share. I believe you know right now if you are going to hire me or not. I am on a limited salary, I have a kid on the way, and I cannot afford to keep flying back and forth between Texas and Michigan.'"

Fred paused for a moment and looked at

John. He shook his head and John saw a faint smile on his face. Fred looked him in the eye and offered John seven hundred and fifty dollars a month. "You *must* be joking," John remarked.

Fred responded matter-of-factly, "I don't joke, John." John was shocked at how low that number was in comparison to some of the other offers from General Motors at the time.

"I needed a little more than seven hundred and fifty dollars so I countered with eight hundred. He then said seven hundred and seventy-five dollars. I wasn't testing my luck, so I stood up, shook his hand, and accepted the position. Esther, the baby, Lisa, and I would now be moving back to my home state of Michigan."

Having been offered the job, John's next step would be to go through the Merrill Lynch training program. The bulk of the training was conducted in New York.

Merrill Lynch ran a year-long training program that was broken up into two parts, with the first part consisting of academic training in New York. There was a school that John attended for three months every day of the week, except for weekends. He remembers, "They had the best instructors in the country on every topic: economics, finance, ratios, you name it. It was a good school. While the training was excellent, they were so cheap, they put five of us in one hotel room. There were four single beds in the living room side-by-side and one in the middle. A guy from North Carolina snored like a freight train; we had to live with it. After class, my roommates found every bar within five miles that served free hors d'oeuvres if they bought a drink. So they would go to these bars, order a beer, and feast on all they could eat. While they went to the bar, I would go back to the hotel and study. I ended up finishing second in my class out of forty-some guys."

The second portion of the training was on-the-job training in Detroit, and that was designed to test John's ability to cope with difficult people and circumstances. "While I was given a first-class academic instruction, I found that going through the on-the-job training program was worse than pledging a fraternity. The brokers treated us trainees like dirt. Most of them were pretty cocky and arrogant, probably because they were making a lot of money. My normal routine was answering phones for brokers, sitting in for secretaries that were out for whatever reason, and running out to get lunch for brokers."

At the start of working at Merrill Lynch, John was located in the Fisher Building in a small space doing little jobs. Joe Deubushy, a fellow worker, stopped by to see him. Joe was tasked with looking up all the phone numbers of potential clients, and he asked John to help. John spent the entire day looking up phone numbers—and getting his white shirts covered in ink. At the time, John only had two suits and two white shirts. Esther would wash his shirt every night to make sure he had a clean one for the following day.

John recalls, "At this point, I came very close to resigning from Merrill Lynch. If I had, I would have gone back to the army." When Joe gave him another set of numbers to look up, John threatened to "beat his ass." Because of this, John had to meet with Fred Picker, his boss, for threatening an employee.

As a result of the meeting with Fred, the next job John was given was to open the unfinished building for the workers every morning and close it every evening. He went beyond the call of duty and proceeded to help those in the building. More importantly, he single-handedly assembled truckloads of furniture while in this position. John needed to prove to Fred that he, as an employee, was worth his position. He needed to prove that he was the hardest-working employee in the building.

Early on, John was living in a one-bedroom apartment with his wife and young daughter. At the time, housing prices were going up 10 percent a year and they couldn't save enough to keep up with inflation. "I was determined to somehow buy a house, and we started looking. Esther was teaching at a middle school in Birmingham, Michigan. The shop teacher that worked with Esther worked part-time as a finish carpenter on weekends. He told her about a house that he started on White Lake.

"He showed us this hole in the ground, and I thought, 'Oh boy.' The mystery is that I told him, 'I only have thirty-two hundred dollars and I can't get a mortgage.' He said, 'Give me the thirty-two hundred dollars as a deposit. If you can't mortgage, I'm not going to have any trouble selling this house, and I will give you your money back.' Before I did that, I called every bank in the city of Detroit, and none of them gave me a mortgage. The house was fifty-six thousand dollars. I wasn't making enough. I couldn't afford the payments, so they wouldn't do it."

At work, Fred Picker approached John and asked, "How are you coming on the mortgage?" John had to explain how he couldn't get one bank in the city of Detroit to give him a mortgage. At that time, Merrill Lynch was the biggest customer of Detroit Bank & Trust (now known as Comerica), depositing tons of money every day of the week. Fred asked , "Have you called Detroit Bank & Trust?"

John said, "Yes, I called this guy in charge of the mortgage department, Bill Miller. When I told him how much money I have and how much I needed, he basically kind of laughed at me."

Fred was disconcerted and said, "I'll be

right back." Five minutes later, John received a phone call from Bill Miller.

John explains, "Bill said, 'How much money do you need? We will finance everything.' And that's how I got my mortgage." This mortgage ended up covering the financing of the house on White Lake, along with the adjacent lot.

Concerned, Esther asked John, "How are we going to afford the payments?" John told her, "I found out it takes eighteen months to repossess a house. So I'm going to make enough in the next eighteen months to be able to afford it, and if I don't, I figure we could probably sell it and make some money on it." Together, John and Esther managed to meet all of the requirements of the loan. John actually encouraged this sort of scrappy and risky thinking process within his broker career. He recalls how he liked his employees to be in debt, because he figured if you're in debt, you're going to work harder to make the money to pay off the debt—which he was right about. "I've been at the house for fifty-two years, I'm still there. I love that house, and I will die there. I totally remodeled it twice. I have never regretted making that kind of investment, and it forced me to work incredibly hard in order to see the payoff.

"I missed the army terribly. Fortunately, I got an offer to join the Department of Army Reserve Unit. I was authorized to pilot an air section that would provide support for the division. At the time, the Army Reserve Unit was approved for an air section, but did not have the means to support it. I had no staff, with the exception of one administrative guy that worked for me. I was given no aircraft, no pilots, and no mechanic. Securing this equipment was important for my role at the base, as I was head of the air section. First, I had to find the equipment, then I could find my staff. The aircrafts were available if you just reached out for them. I was ballsy; I have always been that way. I would call everybody. By writing letters or making phone calls, within a year I had secured everything I needed. For example, I got one aircraft from the boneyard in Arizona. I got another aircraft that had been rebuilt at the Corpus Christi, Texas, airport. Those aircraft had been confiscated for drugs. Soon, I had a hangar full of airplanes. I was very fortunate."

John's broker career spanned forty-eight years. Fred Picker, the first person John reported to during his time at Merrill Lynch, was by far his favorite. His claim to fame was that he caught two touchdown passes as a receiver in the 1955 Rose Bowl. He was a big star and a super nice guy.

"Fred gave me a lot of pointers. He told me that if you work two nights a week and one or two Saturdays a month, you will exceed your contemporaries. I did that: I worked three nights a week until at least 8:00 p.m. and I would go in on Saturdays when I wasn't flying."

When giving advice about the broker business, John tells everyone that he meets, "You are not selling the products, you are selling the confidence that a person has in you. Before I would even walk into a client's office, I'd scan the room. In just five to ten seconds, I'd find something that I have in common with the client. Do they have family, did they go to college, do they like sports? I would start our conversation with that and then let them talk for as long as they wanted. That way, they would feel much more comfortable with me."

So, how did John's work life involving his position at Merrill Lynch as well as his spot at the Department of Army Reserve affect his life at home? Could he maintain the balance necessary between work, fatherhood, and marriage?

CHAPTER 21
THE GRADUATE DIVORCE

I work as an optimal performance psychologist. I chose to do that because I didn't want to deal exclusively with issues related to divorce, suicide, and stress-related problems. I wanted to focus my career on helping people to achieve optimal performance on whatever field of play they may be engaged in. However, I soon found that it doesn't matter if I am working with professional athletes, entertainers, or top-echelon executives, they all go through the same challenges in their families and with their friends as anyone else, including divorces, suicides, and other difficult human challenges. Whenever I help a couple through a divorce, I make it perfectly clear that I don't care if they stay together or get a divorce; I am in the mental health business, and I want them to do what is best for them in that respect. One of the common themes in long-term marriages that end in divorce is what I will call "the graduate divorce." Specifically, when the kids leave the nest, the parents realize that the children were the bond that held them together, even during times when they thought about separating. In essence, this was the case with John and Esther.

There was no question that Esther valued John's work ethic and ability to generate a good income. She remembers stuffing envelopes to generate business for John in his Merrill Lynch role. During his time with Merrill Lynch, John was also working as a helicopter pilot at Selfrage Air Force Base, so he was gone a great deal of the time. During the twenty years of working at Merrill Lynch and being involved with various Army Reserve opportunities, Esther was evolving in her own career of education and pursuing her own career goals simultaneously. Within this time period, each party realized that they were moving in opposite directions from each other, and their children had kept them focused on one shared goal of parenthood.

"You can prepare for combat, but you cannot prepare for the emotions of a divorce," said John. "Esther is a good person, but getting a divorce was probably the best thing for the both of us at the time."

When asked about her mother, John and Esther's second daughter, Lauri, said, "Mom was and still is a great mother. She was very involved in our sports, school activities, friends, and trips with Dad. If I had to choose one word to describe my mother, it would be 'supportive.' She always made sure that things were going well for us daughters, whether it be with school, friends, etc. Mom, my sister, and I all worked at staying in shape, maintaining a good diet, exercise, etc. We completed three marathons together, including the Chicago Marathon. My mom is also very intellectual and speaks three different languages: English, Spanish, and French. She loves to travel and we have traveled internationally together quite a bit. We have been to Spain,

Australia, and Italy. Mom dated a few guys after the divorce, but never remarried. She now resides in Florida and enjoys being involved in charity work."

About her father, she said, "Dad was always a very good provider and took a big interest in taking the whole family on trips to Disney World and doing other things that were fun for us as kids. He has been a really great grandfather to my boys."

When looking at the eventual divorce between Esther and John, it seemed appropriate to talk to Keith Charters. It is safe to say that Keith Charters is John's best friend. From their high school years through today, they have shared many personal and professional experiences. In light of this, I asked Keith and his wife Caroline about Esther, because while they currently share a close relationship with John and his wife Carole, they have also maintained a close relationship with Esther after John and Esther's divorce.

When I asked Keith and Caroline about Esther, they affirmed that Esther was a very good mother and school teacher. Fellow educators and her students had high respect for her performance. She has always been very active in the community. She has served as president of the Professional Education Organization (PEO).

Both John and Esther have gone on to live full lives.

CHAPTER 22
THUMBS UP

The statement "No man left behind" is simple and clear. It is based on the idea that every member of a military unit is critical to the success of the mission. If a soldier is wounded, lost, or captured, the unit must make every effort to recover or reclaim them, even if it puts other members of the unit at risk.

The impact of the deeply rooted commitment of "No man left behind" surfaced one day unexpectedly when John was having some remodeling done on the house he would return to after his divorce. He had been living in a condo while Esther and he were separated. The house decor was dominated by dark carpets and cabinets, and John wanted to change the look and feel by featuring the color white. This included the closet cabinets.

John hired a closet builder recommended by the contractor who was doing much of the remodeling work on John's house. He said, "Tim Whipple is a respected craftsman I know and all he is doing now is closets and cabinets. Tim's work is reasonably priced and he does a great job."

Tim turned out to be very skilled. He measured all the cabinets, drawers, and closets in the house. As John observed his work, he couldn't help but notice that every time he turned around, Tim was staring at him.

A couple of days later, Tim called John and said, "I forgot to measure the closets in your bedrooms and rec room. Can I meet you there one night?"

When they met later that week, John noticed that, once more, he was being stared at. Tim finally said, "Can I ask you a question? Were you in the army?"

John replied, "Yes."

Tim asked, "Vietnam of the Twenty-Fifth Division?"

Confused, John said, "Yes, how did you know that?"

Tim answered, "You saved my life. I was shot up and near death. You came in the middle of the night, got me into the helicopter."

John then replied, "You know, I don't remember this, but I hardly remember the faces of a lot of guys that I flew with. How can you remember my face from thirty years ago?"

He said, "I will tell you why. First, when you think you're dying, you don't forget. Secondly, when they threw me in the back of that Huey, I knew I was dying. You looked at me, and you gave me a thumbs-up. Your gesture gave me the hope that I was going to survive."

John was astonished by what Tim had said, because he believed that he was the only guy that gave the thumbs-up gesture to encourage wounded warriors. When they threw men into the back of the Huey, shot up real bad, John would always look at them and give them a thumbs-up, encouraging them to hang on, and that he would get them safely back to base.

This thumbs-up gesture just reminded John of the value of holding dear the motto, "No man left behind."

CHAPTER 23

MARRIAGE: THE SECOND TIME AROUND

Carole was hired by Merrill Lynch on September 5, 1980, as a sales assistant for four brokers. After going back to school and many hours of on-the-job training, she received her brokerage license in 1987. She then became a broker and eventually was asked by John to join his team in 2005. At that time, John was the only broker at Merrill Lynch that had a real team. Other brokers would have affiliations between themselves, but not on a permanent basis.

John and Carole became friends in June of 1985. John invited Carole and her husband to go to a Detroit Red Wings hockey game. After that night, the two couples would get together for various events. John and Esther divorced in 1990 and Carole and her husband divorced shortly after.

According to Carole, "John and I started dating in 2005. We were married September 5, 2010, in a civil ceremony by his Army Reserve chaplain, Cleven Jones. We 'remarried' again in October of 2010 at Holy Spirit Catholic Church in Highland, Michigan."

Carole describes her husband in glowing terms. Professionally, she sees him as a gifted, talented, "real-deal" stock broker. He has used his God-given talent to benefit so many people, and he also expanded that gift to speaking about and educating other brokers on how to be successful: client first before self. John is an excellent mentor and still mentors when called upon.

Carole shares that, on a personal level, "if John were to have a vulnerability, it would be that he is overly trusting. He trusts everyone to a fault. To me personally, his most valued asset is his sense of humor. He is loving, romantic, and loves people, things, God, his family, and his country."

John loves being a father and grandfather to their fifteen grandchildren, ages fifteen to thirty-five. John has four, and Carole has eleven, and he loves them all equally. He is their grandpa.

"In summary," Carole says, "John is unique, the epitome of class, a true gentleman, the best husband in the world, considerate, and generous to an extreme. I am so very proud to be his wife!"

When asked about Carole, the very first comment John says is, "Anybody who knows Carole can see that she is authentic. She is true to her own personality, values, and spirit—regardless of the pressure she is under to act otherwise. If my life was a ship, Carole would be the anchor that holds me in place, and the sails that take me through life's journey."

John adds, "I don't need the whole world to love me, I just need one person, and I'm happy to say that Carole is that person. My life's greatest achievement is that I get to be with her nearly every day. I am always glad to see her come home and sad to see her leave."

Carole and John enjoy doing things together and, at the same time, they readily let each other pursue their different interests without interference. Carole and John's marriage works because they trust that they will look out for each other if something were to happen in the future. And, after all these years together, they still have great physical chemistry.

As I have observed John and Carole in many different settings, I can see there is no "me-first" in their relationship. For example, John loves to entertain. Carole organizes, cooks, cleans up, etc. She never complains. On the other hand, John willingly engages in efforts important to Carole, such as delivering Meals on Wheels to elderly and homebound people.

Perhaps the most interesting phase of John and Carole's marriage happened after he retired from Merrill Lynch in 2018. From that point forward, they worked as a team supporting each other's wants and needs, and contributing to their shared goal of enriching the lives of others.

PART IV:

AS PAUL HARVEY USED TO SAY, "AND NOW, FOR THE REST OF THE STORY!"

Radio broadcaster Paul Harvey used to say at the end of each show, "And now, for the rest of the story." He would then surprise the listener with an added comment or two that would amaze or fascinate. John's pathway in life after the military and Merrill Lynch adds dimension to John's story. So now, for the rest of John's story.

CHAPTER 24
FOLLOWING IN MOM'S FOOTSTEPS

John's generativity can justifiably be traced to the giving nature of his mother. While she ran her small grocery store, she extended credit even when she suspected she would never get paid.

John amassed a great deal of wealth while heading his investment team at Merrill Lynch. He did this by changing the culture at Merrill Lynch through shifting their existing individual mode of operation to a team-oriented approach, patterned after his military experience in Vietnam. His team members were expected to master their jobs but also to support one another in ways that protected individuals from losing a client. As in most competitive businesses, you sometimes lose clients. But John always coached his brokers from the perspective, "We cannot lose. We win—or we learn."

John received the following letter from the national sales director at Merrill Lynch:

DON STEELE, PH.D

Andrew M. Sieg
Managing Director
Head of Merrill Lynch Wealth Management
Merrill Lynch, Pierce, Fenner & Smith

December 18, 2018

Mr. John G. Kulhavi
Kulhavi Wealth Management Team
Merrill Lynch
39001 West 12 Mile Road
Farmington Hills, MI 48331

Dear John:

I'm pleased to join with your colleagues in Michigan and across the country in saluting you as you celebrate an extraordinary tour of duty – more than 43 years – as one of Merrill Lynch's most extraordinary Financial Advisors.

The amazing team you've built has achieved exceptional performance - $1.5 billion in AUM and $11 million in production credits through a largely fee-based business. Personally, you've earned more than your share of industry accolades – consistently named a member of Barron' Top Financial Advisors, both nationally and locally in Michigan. Most importantly, your embrace of goals-based, personalized client service, long before it became popular, has given you client satisfaction ratings approaching 100 percent.

You've brought a remarkable background to your career in wealth management. As a Vietnam helicopter pilot in close combat, you were awarded some of the nation's highest military decorations for your refusal to leave no man behind. That integrity of character has played through in your continued service in the Army Reserves and through your many charitable endeavors on behalf of veterans as well as your beloved alma mater, Central Michigan University.

I've heard that Don Regan, our late Chairman and CEO, gave you his personal authorization to form a team when you started out four decades ago. I can imagine him smiling down on you today as he sees what you've built over the years. A true pioneer – and consummate team leader in your own right. I think Mr. Regan would agree with all of us – colleagues, clients and friends everywhere – that you've earned one final accolade: *legend*!

We are all grateful to you, John. And as you embark on new adventures, we wish you and your family all the best that life has to offer. You've earned it.

Sincerely,

One Bryant Park, 50th Floor New York, NY 10036
T 646.855.22
andy.sieg@ml.com

Are Not FDIC Insured	Are Not Bank Guaranteed	May Lose Value

John retained his affiliation with Merrill Lynch until December of 2018, serving forty-eight years as a financial advisor.

As John moved forward with his life, he followed the pathway laid out in the following poem, entitled "Build a Better World" (anonymous).

> *"Build a better world," said God*
> *And I answered "How?*
> *The world is such a vast place*
> *So complicated now*
> *And I am small and simple*
> *There's little I can do."*
> *And God in all his wisdom said,*
> *"Just build a better you."*

In his heart of hearts, John wanted to do well with his money but he also wanted to do good with it. His generativity showed up in many unpredictable and adventurous ways. His friend Keith Charters had this to say about John: "John has always been good at earning money, but there is another side to John. He is always willing to share the riches. I can say without reservation that he is the most generous person I have ever met."

In the stories that follow, I will briefly try to capture what drove John's spirit of intent to give freely and unstintingly. John exercises a warm-hearted readiness to help others fulfill their dreams by offering financial assistance and mentoring.

As John's generosity is the thread that runs through his later years in life, it is important to note that John has never lost sight of the fact that to give generously, you must generate and sustain significant wealth. John has made and continues to make business investments. He is an angel investor for aspiring entrepreneurs.

An angel investor is typically one person who provides capital in early-stage startups or small businesses in exchange for equity in the company. Sometimes referred to as accredited investors, angel investors are high-net-worth individuals. The US Securities and Exchange Commission reserves the use of the label of accredited investor to those who have a net worth of one million dollars or more. John is an accredited angel investor, frequently providing much-needed cash infusions to help businesses down the path to profitability.

John's friends and business associates agree that when it comes to business investments, John is challenged by taking something that is broken and trying to make it better than it ever was before. Many people ask him, "Why do you get involved in these endeavors?" John would answer, "That is what drives me, I don't know why."

John currently is the sole owner or partner in seventeen varied businesses. His usual approach is to invest in an individual who is serving as the manager or who plans to serve as the manager. John does not want to manage any of his businesses.

While most of John's angel investing has produced good results, his overly trusting nature has, on occasion, cost him money and tarnished relationships.

In addition to investing in people and organizations, John also donates much of his financial wealth to organizations and charities that he holds closest to his heart.

When it comes to his largest charitable contribution, Central Michigan University tops John's list. He is currently the largest living donor to CMU. He has donated, in total, about nine million dollars.

John is a big believer in his alma mater. He contributed about five million dollars to the CMU neuroscience program. During that time, the program was directed by Dr. Gary

Dunbar. About five years ago, the National Society for Neuroscience evaluated every collegiate-level neuroscience program in the country. This prestigious organization rated CMU's neuroscience program the best in the United States. CMU beat the programs at other colleges such as Harvard, Princeton, MIT, the University of Michigan, and every other university at an overall level. John's contribution and Gary's leadership played significant roles in CMU winning this coveted neuroscience award.

Historically, a quarter to a half of John's CMU donations would go to the neuroscience program. Now, John gives another 25 percent to the ROTC, and the remainder goes to CMU athletics. John's favorite sports are women's basketball and men's wrestling and baseball because they have the greatest need and show the most appreciation for his gifts.

A couple of years ago, John was informed by CMU's assistant athletic director, Davis Craigwell, that the women's track team had no donors at all. John started donating money to them. Afterwards, John was informed that they used part of the money to buy a pole for the women's pole vaulters. That weekend, they set a new Mid-American Conference (MAC) record using the pole that John donated to them.

John has also been a strong contributor to military veteran organizations and causes. For example, he headed the funding drive under Former Governor John Engler in Michigan to build a monument and the Veteran's State Park in front of the Hall of Justice building in Lansing, Michigan. John continues to give to various veterans associations such as the Wounded Warrior Project, the American Legion, Vietnam Veterans of America, and more.

John currently has seventeen operating businesses in which he is either the sole owner or a partner. If John's mother were looking down on his actions today, she would be incredibly proud of the giving nature that she passed on to John, and that he exercises every day.

CHAPTER 25
THE OLDER I GET

John Kulhavi lives what most would call a luxurious life. He and Carole can literally get almost anything they want. They have the home John has lived in for fifty years on White Lake in Michigan. They also have a beautiful ocean property in Cape Coral, Florida, that is decorated with a variety of military and entertainment artifacts as well as pictures that John has gathered over the years.

Additionally, John has his one-thousand-acre Horny Hollow Hunting Haven, located in Curran, Michigan. The property, originally purchased and co-owned with four other partners in 1971, is now entirely in

John's name. At this private camp, John and Carole have worked together over the years to create an atmosphere filled with activities they and their family truly enjoy. For example, Horny Hollow consists of ten miles of pathways for off-road riding, a go-kart track, a bocce ball field, trap and rifle ranges, and a miniature golf course.

John's favorite thing to do, according to Carole, is to watch others having fun. Having been raised in the small, remote town of Skidway Lake, he remembers how difficult it was for him and others similarly situated to experience the fun and excitement of attending state fairs, playing golf, and other fun activities. He decided to create his own place with multiple options to provide fun opportunities for parents and their children at really affordable family rates.

Furthermore, John regularly hosts military veterans, police officers, and first responders at the property. On site, John has quite a few displays and military vehicles showcased, including a Huey helicopter similar to one that John flew in Vietnam. Frequently, these groups of people visiting Horny Hollow suffer from PTSD. The veterans and first responders both truly enjoy the campsite and all of its offerings. Additionally, John has offered the property and its amenities to professors and instructors of CMU's ROTC program before the school year begins each fall for the past few summers. It provides a way for the staff to recharge and spend some much-deserved time away with their families.

The Kulhavis spend a great deal of time hosting guests and entertaining people from all walks of life on the Horny Hollow property. John is a hunter, and he loves to host others to hunt on his property, so they have really nice accommodations and are virtually assured of scoring a trophy deer or bird.

Perhaps John's greatest legacy is how he has expanded the entertainment, camping, and other possibilities in and around his Horny Hollow Hunting Haven. He has grown his entertainment offerings for fun and recreation to include the Cedar Valley RV Park, Cedar Valley Golf Course, the Pines Golf Course of Fairview, and the second-largest privately-owned amusement park in the state of Michigan, Cedar Valley's Wild Frontier Fun Park. Each of the properties listed are about eighteen miles away from the Horny Hollow Hunting Haven property. The amusement park offers rides and entertainment to visitors who tend to live in remote areas and frequently have below-average incomes and limited funds for recreational-type spending. Because of these things, John charges entry and ride fees that are far below that of a state fair or similar experience. He even has two go-kart tracks—one for young kids and one for older kids.

John has patterned his life after a quote by Theodore Roosevelt, America's twenty-sixth president: "Speak softly and carry a big stick." Roosevelt also made another profound statement: "Far better it is to dare mighty things, to win glorious triumphs, even though checkered by failure, than to rank with those poor spirits who neither enjoy nor suffer much, because they live in the gray twilight that knows not victory nor defeat." John says that this quote describes his life's philosophy. He would rather take a risk than not try at all—even if he may fail the first time around. This attitude is evident in many of his business endeavors, and has proven to be a successful strategy.

Now, I must also recognize John Kulhavi's love of humor. No matter how dire the straits, he can laugh and make others laugh. For example, when John gave the commencement address at Central Michigan University one year, he delighted the faculty and students with these closing remarks:

> In 1987, the University of Michigan psychology department conducted a study, the purpose of which was to determine the comprehension of an audience of young adults given by a speaker on virtually any topic. The following results revealed that 25 percent, a quarter of the audience, paid reasonably close attention and could accurately relate the main theme of the presentation. Another 25 percent could not accurately relate the main theme. The remaining 50 percent, half the audience of young adults, within seconds of the start of the presentation, immediately began having sexual fantasies and remained in that mode for the rest of the pre-

sentation. So, I'm very happy that I brought so much pleasure to so many of you.

John got a standing ovation!

The song, "The Older I Get," written by Alan Jackson, appears to capture John's thinking right now:

> *The older I get, the more I think*
> *You only get a minute, better live*
>   *while you're in it*
> *Cause it's gone in a blink*
> *And the older I get,*
> *the truer it is*
> *It's the people you love, not the*
>   *money and stuff*
> *That makes you rich*
> *And if they found a fountain of*
>   *youth,*
> *I wouldn't drink a drop and that's*
>   *the truth*
> *Funny how it feels I'm just getting to my best years yet*

The older I get
The fewer friends I have
But you don't need a lot when the ones you've got
Have always got your back
And the older I get
The better I am
At knowing when to give
And when to just not give a damn
And if they found a fountain of youth,
I wouldn't drink a drop and that's the truth
Funny how it feels I'm just getting to my best years yet
And I don't mind all the lines
From all the times I've laughed and cried
Souvenirs and little signs of the life I've lived
The older I get
The longer I pray
I don't know why, I guess that I've
Got more to say
And the older I get
The more thankful I feel

*For the life I've had and all the life
I'm living still*

This book captures the life and times of Retired Brigadier General John G. Kulhavi. Of all of the legacy books I have written, this one stands out. It is a true story of the emergence of a relatively poor but industrious young child who grew into a highly decorated military warrior, a world-class financial advisor, a serial entrepreneur, and a very generous philanthropist. Through all of this, he has remained humble and lives a life of gratitude. His mantra in life is, "I cannot lose. I will win—or I will learn."

COMMENDATIONS

ABOUT JOHN:

Lorem ipsum dolor sit amet, consectetur adipiscing elit, sed do eiusmod tempor incididunt ut labore et dolore magna aliqua. Ut enim ad minim veniam, quis nostrud exercitation ullamco laboris nisi ut aliquip ex ea commodo consequat. Duis aute irure dolor in reprehenderit in voluptate velit esse cillum dolore eu fugiat nulla pariatur. Excepteur sint occaecat cupidatat non proident, sunt in culpa qui officia deserunt mollit anim id est laborum.

Lorem ipsum dolor sit amet, consectetur adipiscing elit, sed do eiusmod tempor incididunt ut labore et dolore magna aliqua. Ut enim ad minim veniam, quis nostrud exercitation ullamco laboris nisi ut aliquip ex ea commodo consequat.

Duis aute irure dolor in reprehenderit in voluptate velit esse cillum dolore eu fugiat nulla pariatur. Excepteur sint occaecatcupidatat non proident, sunt in culpa qui officia deserunt mollit anim id est laborum.

ABOUT THE AUTHOR

Dr. Don Steele is the president of Performance Learning, Inc.—the optimal performance coaching and consulting enterprise he founded in 1987. One essential component of Performance Learning, Inc., in addition to coaching, speaking, and conducting seminars, is capturing the lives and times of ordinary people who have done extraordinary things in what is called *The Legacy Book Series.* Several books from his series are now available via Barnes and Noble, Amazon, and PLI:

- *Undefeated:* The true story of how the family-owned Shepler's Mackinac Island Ferry Service survived and advanced through three generations.
- *Rebel Without Applause:* A story that captures the life and times of Jon D. Hall, founder and CEO of the family-owned and

operated Glastender, Inc., a very successful food equipment manufacturing business located in Saginaw, Michigan.

- *The Misfit Millionaire:* The course of this book relates the progress of Terry Duperon's life while pursuing his dream of becoming a successful inventor. His success was accomplished despite his being limited by his inability to read or write due to severe dyslexia.

According to author Lawrence Allen, "Dr. Don Steele's writing style is that of a fiction storyteller, but crafted with the gravity of a news reporter."

Made in the USA
Monee, IL
15 September 2024

65836317R20118